Routemasters
AROUND GREAT BRITAIN

Steve Fennell

Blackpool 527 (RM879) passes the North Pier on Beachroamer 55.
(Steve Fennell)

Contents

ISBN 0 9509910 6 6

Published by DPR Marketing & Sales (The World of Transport), 37 Heath Road, Twickenham, Middlesex TW1 4AW

Printed by The Ludo Press Ltd, London SW18 3DG

© DPR Marketing & Sales (The World of Transport) November 1988

I would like to express my thanks to the many people who have contributed to this book. In particular Ian Manning of Clydeside Scottish, Sholto Thomas of Strathtay Scottish, John Lidstone of Southend Transport and John Young of Greater Manchester Buses who have all gone out of their way to supply details of their own company's operations and, in some cases, those of others as well! Thanks are also due to the contributing photographers, many of whom have supplied material at very short notice, not helped by the recent turmoil within the postal industry. Finally, I would like to pass on my appreciation to George Watson, Clydeside Scottish's General Manager, for providing the most thought-provoking foreword on page 3. It is the author's humble opinion that the RM operations of Clydeside are the most interesting in the country, even more so than in the Routemaster's birthplace of London. I would recommend a visit to Clydeside territory to anyone!

Please note that in the 'route working' lists that follow in each individual heading, only the *section* of route that sees Routemaster operation is listed. In some cases the full route is considerably longer.

Additionally, it should be noted that this book only deals with former London Routemasters in PSV service. Preserved and privately owned examples are not included.

STEVE FENNELL

November 1988

Foreword

My first encounter with the Routemaster was on a wet day in 1960 when as a young enthusiast I travelled on Service 5 immediately following the stage IV Barking Road trolleybus conversions.

Somehow, despite living at this time in Colindale, I contrived to miss Routemasters working from Cricklewood and elsewhere, so this experience in East London was new and to me rare.

Reeking newness, the Routemaster scored an immediate success with me despite a curious lack of ventilation in the prime front top deck position.

Subsequent months and years saw my attentions concentrating on seeing new and even higher numbers as the large trolleybus fleet contracted in the face of the all-conquering Routemaster.

I particularly remember the penultimate trolleybus conversion when on a bitterly cold morning I stood waiting for seemingly hours at Burnt Oak Broadway for my first sight of a gleaming new Routemaster on the 245 or 266. It all seemed most unreal but eventually the first Routemaster did arrive. The change was accepted as positive progress although the pall of smoke over Colindale indicated the loss of a close childhood friend.

Around 25 years later, and now a transport manager in the brave new world of deregulated, competitive bus operation, it was hard to believe that those same Routemasters were about to enter their second (?) Indian summer, and often in places undreamt of all those years ago.

The very factors which caused the creation of the ultimate traditional British bus had conspired to re-emerge again in 1986 as the public transport industry swung emphatically back in favour of the customer and market awareness.

Of course these were precisely the factors that inspired the design of the Routemaster, and its illustrious forebearers whose history can be directly traced back to the early days of bus competition and private bus operators.

When new the Routemaster was rumoured to have cost as much as 50% more than contemporary models, but this investment has paid off handsomely in terms of longevity, crew and passenger acceptability.

With a mechanical specification, quality of construction and economy which manufacturers can only surpass with difficulty today, together with a standard of ride and comfort which is the envy of many a manufacturer of 'tin boxes', the Routemaster still commands considerable respect in the industry.

For these reasons it can come as little surprise to many that operators outside London and preservationists are queuing up to acquire surplus Routemasters for further commercial use or just plain 'fun'.

In Scotland, where competition remains extremely fierce since deregulation, once again the virtues of the Routemaster shine brightly. Economy, speed of loading in city operations, sprightly performance and high passenger popularity have already given the Routemaster a place in Scottish bus history alongside other former members of the London Transport family including Guy and RT types.

Meanwhile Routemaster developments continue apace with DAF and IVECO engine versions being added to the familiar AEC and Leyland ranks. New trims, brash liveries and other technical improvements are all helping to ensure that the Routemaster will stay on our streets for some years yet. A tribute indeed to the past skills of AEC and Park Royal.

Throughout Britain, and indeed the world, the Routemaster is respected, revered and retained as a symbol of quintessential London-ness and British-ness, which may perhaps be summed up as solid, dependable and friendly.

The accents (or languages) may be different but the effect is the same for all who travel by Routemaster bus.

Long may it remain!

G. I. WATSON,

General Manager, Clydeside Scottish Omnibuses Ltd

Stagecoach/Magicbus

The 'Routemasters around Great Britain' story really begins in Scotland, when in January 1985 a local Perth operator, 'Stagecoach Ltd', purchased five standard RMs from London buses for use on local services around Perth and Dundee. A further five Routemasters followed in May whilst the following year yet another five buses were obtained. All of these early purchases were Leyland engined vehicles, although later purchases have brought buses with AEC units into stock. Subsequently a number of these early acquisitions were scrapped and used as a source of spare parts whilst one bus was exchanged with a preservationist for a former Northern General front entrance Routemaster.

The deregulation of local stage carriage service from 26 October 1986 saw Stagecoach enter the brave new deregulated bus fracas in Glasgow from D Day itself. Three services were registered linking Glasgow City Centre with East Kilbride, Easterhouse and Castlemilk numbered 18, 19 and 20 respectively. All of the Routemasters obtained so far were transferred to a newly formed Stagecoach subsidary company trading as 'Magicbus', which was set up specifically to operate these new services. Whilst the 18 and 19 were normally operated by a motley collection of coaches and Bristol Loddekkas with the occasional Routemaster, the 20 became a 100% RM operation, due to the fact that the police wouldn't allow any larger vehicles to operate over the proposed routing in the vast Castlemilk Estate.

The East Kilbride service failed to come up to expectations and was withdrawn from 24 January 1987. At the same time the Easterhouse service was doubled in frequency and generally converted to Routemaster operation. A further addition to the route network was made the following summer when Magicbus were awarded a contract by Strathclyde PTE for an evening service between Castlemilk and Bridgeton Cross. Numbered 22, the occasional Routemaster could also be found on this service.

As well as being the first operator outside London to take Routemasters, Stagecoach were also the first to start the irritating habit of re-registering their RMs which carried non-suffix marks. RMs 504 and 560 were the first to be re-registered, appearing in 1986 carrying EDS-A registrations. The former London numbers either being sold or transferred to other company associated vehicles. At the time of writing nine Stagecoach Routemasters (including one ex-Northern example) have been so treated, the latest being RM831 which was undertaken during summer 1988.

The privatisation of the National Bus Company gave Stagecoach the opportunity for expansion and over a relatively short period of time three former NBC companies. Hampshire Bus, Cumberland Motor Services and United Counties came under Stagecoach control. Of these new acquisitions, Cumberland and United Counties were to see Routemaster operation themselves in the not too distant future and details of these fleets can be found under their respective headings later in this book.

The Stagecoach purchase of Hampshire Bus brought with it another area of severe competition amongst bus operators, namely Southampton. Routemasters were subsequently introduced to this town by Southampton City Bus (see page 37) who themselves were experiencing severe competition with the Solent Blue Line subsidary of Southern Vectis. Soon after the Hampshire Bus acquisition Stagecoach purchased another batch of Routemasters (ten RMs and one RMA) and immediately sent them to the former Hampshire Bus Overhaul Works at Barton Park, causing in the process a considerable amount of speculation as to their intended use. However, in a surprise move Stagecoach sold off the Southampton operations to Southern Vectis and concurrent with the sale was the transfer of these additional Routemasters to Scottish based premises. So ended an extremely interesting saga which no doubt caused a certain amount of concern within the offices of various other operators within the Southampton area!

Yet more RMs were obtained in November 1987, and, along with the rumoured Hampshire Bus batch, were used to enhance the Magicbus presence in Glasgow. Route 19 was extended across Glasgow to Milton whilst another service, numbered 25, was introduced providing an additional link between the City Centre and Castlemilk. Both of these extensions brought Magicbus into further competition with 'Strathclyde's Buses', the former Strathclyde PTE Company, and their reaction was as swift as it was predictable. Needless to say Magicbus terminated these new operations after only a few months and their route pattern, at least as far as the sphere of RM operation was concerned, reverted to the pre-November 1987 position.

One minor change, concurrent with the withdrawal of these services was the resiting of the route 19 terminus in Glasgow to St George's Square. Prior to the Milton extension the 19's terminus had been tucked away in a corner of Buchanan Street Bus Station. No doubt it was felt that a more central terminal would be more conducive to increased passenger loadings.

Since the acquisition of Routemasters commenced in January 1985 some 37 standard RMs have been obtained along with two of the ex-British Airways RMA type and four ex-Northern General front entrance specimens. Of the 37 standard RMs one (1571) was, as detailed previously, used to obtain a Northern General example (included in the Northern total above), one (504) had been transferred to the Stagecoach United Counties fleet, whilst another (1741) has passed to an independent operator. One has passed to a preservationist (1250), whilst at least two (703 and 1847), possibly others, have been scrapped, in the process providing a float of spare parts. For completeness it perhaps should be mentioned that two of the former Northern vehicles have been withdrawn, one completely written off by fire damage, whilst the other encountered a low bridge in its travels. Although repair of this latter example was proposed, further accident damage appears to have precluded this!

The actual operational fleet seems to fluctuate regularly and although 35 different Routemaster vehicles remain in stock, the actual vehicle requirements for the Glasgow based operation are considerably less. Stagecoach have extensive storage ground at Spittalfield near Perth and it is known that a handful of Routemasters are stored at this location. Some stored RMs can also be found, at the time of writing, at Cumberland Motor Services Keswick Bus Station.

Stagecoach/Magicbus services which see scheduled Routemaster operation

19: Glasgow City Centre–M8 Motorway–
Easterhouse Circular
(Mon.–Sat., not evenings, partial operation only)

20: Glasgow City Centre–Castlemilk Circular
(Daily operation, evenings included)

22: Castlemilk–Bridgeton Cross
(Mon.–Sat. evening operation,
very occasionally Routemaster operated)

* indicates that bus carries early body with non opening front upper deck windows.

Stagecoach/Magicbus Routemaster Fleetlist

RM Bonnet Number	Current Registration Number	Original Registration Number
RMA20	NMY633E	–
RMA50	NMY634E	–
RM43	EDS247A	VLT43
RM223*	WTS177A	VLT223
RM560	EDS50A	WLT560
RM667	EDS143A	WLT667
RM831	EDS341A	WLT831
RM909	WLT909	–
RM938	WLT938	–
RM1056	56CLT	–
RM1087	87CLT	–
RM1145	145CLT	–
RM1164	164CLT	–
RM1245	245CLT	–
RM1274	274CLT	–
RM1289	289CLT	–
RM1397	397CLT	–
RM1449	449CLT	–
RM1596	EDS146A	596CLT
RM1599	YTS820A	599CLT
RM1601	601DYE	–
RM1602	602DYE	–
RM1607	607DYE	–
RM1611	EDS129A	611DYE
RM1628	628DYE	–
RM1699	699DYE	–
RM1838	838DYE	–
RM1858	858DYE	–
RM1968	ALD968B	–
RM2063	ALM63B	–
RM2121	CUV121C	–

Early days of the Magicbus operation see RM1607 at the St Enoch's Square terminus in Glasgow. *(Steve Fennell)*

Daylight hours at St Enoch's Square produce RM1599 (reregistered YTS820A) and RM43 (reregistered EDS247A). The former vehicle is being used for crew ferry purposes. *(Steve Fennell)*

RM1087 turns from Dixon Street into St Enoch's Square at the end of its journey from Castlemilk. Most surprisingly, the majority of the Stagecoach Routemaster fleet still retain their London registration numbers. *(Steve Fennell)*

One bus which has been registered is RM831, now masquerading as EDS341A. This bus, at the time of writing, is the most recent Magicbus example to be so treated and is illustrated here entering Dixon Street. *(Steve Fennell)*

The other Magicbus RM service is the 19 which links Glasgow with Easterhouse. At one stage the route operated across Glasgow to Milton but this projection has since been withdrawn. Carrying the through destination blind for the Milton extension, RM1628 is seen in Glasgow City Centre. *(Russell Upcraft)*

Carrying the more usual 'Express' display, **RM1449** is seen at St George's Square, Glasgow. *(Russell Upcraft)*

Magicbus have two RMAs in their fleet, one of which has been fitted with full destination blind equipment from a withdrawn standard RM. RMA20 is seen at the Magicbus Depot in Glasgow. *(Russell Upcraft)*

Clydeside Scottish Omnibus Co. Ltd

The Clydeside Routemaster story can be traced back to July 1985 when RM652 was borrowed and placed on display at the company's open day at Paisley Depot. Following the open day the bus was evaluated in service at all Clydeside garages and was joined by a further example from London in August. During August RM652 was purchased and, along with the newly arrived RM694, entered service from Paisley Depot. Shortly afterwards RM652 was repainted into full Clydeside livery of red and yellow and, although technically still on loan, 694 was afforded the same treatment in October. Seeing the re-introduction of crew operation as an effective weapon in which to combat deregulation the following October, Clydeside ordered a substantial number of Routemasters. Initial arrivals entered service at Paisley and Inchinnan Depots whilst some were lent to Scottish Bus Group members Kelvin and Strathtay for evaluation, these operators also seeing the merits of crew operation. Both of these companies were subsequently to take sizeable quantities of RMs. What further added the London flavour to the Clydeside fleet was the use of full London style destination blinds supplied initially by the now closed LT Aldenham Works and latterly by the premises at Chiswick in West London, now part of the Frontsource Group.

On introduction at Paisley and Inchinnan Depots, the RMs were restricted in the main to local work in and around Paisley and Renfrew and it was not until the spring of 1986 that sufficient vehicles were available to enable an allocation to be made at Johnstone Depot. Initially, these were also restricted to local work but very soon the occasional Routemaster could be seen making the sortie to Glasgow City along the Paisley Road on the busy 636/8/9 group of services. As the number of vehicles available increased so did their use and by August 1986 six RMs a day were to be found plying back and forth between Johnstone and Glasgow. Service revisions from September 1986 saw a mass increase in Routemaster requirements by Clydeside. Almost all of the daytime Paisley Road service was Routemaster operated, more than doubling overnight Johnstone Depot's RM allocation. At the same time the routes were renumbered into two digit fashion, in the main dropping the 600 series number. i.e. 636 became 36, etc.

Still Routemasters were being taken into stock and from D Day, 26 October, Thornliebank Depot became the fourth Clydeside establishment to receive an RM allocation when routes 10 and 11 were introduced, running from Darnley and Carnwandric across Glasgow to Balornock East providing a joint five minute headway.

Subsequent changes to the crew network since D Day have been of a 'fine tuning' nature rather than any wholesale route restructuring, which suggests that Clydeside 'got it right' in the first place, unlike some other operators in Glasgow whose services always seem to be in a state of turmoil!

Originally the Routemasters were given fleet numbers from 251 upwards, and an attempt was made to match at least part of the registration number with the proposed fleet number. Fleet numbers, incidentally, were carried in the former running number holders on each side of the vehicles giving those used to London tradition the impression that running numbers were in use. However, this scheme soon fell from favour and it was subsequently decided to identify the buses by their existing London RM fleet numbers; this practice has remained to the present day.

To their credit, Clydeside have avoided the temptation of re-registering the fleet and transferring the dateless original RM registrations to other vehicles. The only registration to have been so used being VLT28 (RM28) off of a scrap vehicle. With such a large fleet the scope for variety is perhaps inevitable and as early as summer 1986 one Routemaster was the subject of livery experiments. RM697 was finished in a 'Kelvin' style livery with a large yellow wedge front. Fortunately, this version was rejected, the bus never seeing public service in this guise, being repainted into the more restrained version of Clydeside's colours prior to entering service from Thornliebank Depot.

Two vehicles currently carry special advertisement liveries. RM17 is an overall advert for 'Westcars', a local SAAB dealer. Finished in a white and blue based livery, the bus is allocated to Thornliebank Depot and spends most of its time on routes 10 and 11. The second vehicle, RM694, carries a 'wrap-round' scheme for Balfour Beatty Homes. This bus is currently allocated to Paisley Depot and normally operates on routes 21 and 24. One bus which used to carry a special livery but has since reverted to normal fleet colours was RM416. This bus carried a half-n-half London/Clydeside livery specifically to promote the Aberlour Children in Need Appeal. It was repainted back to normal fleet livery in April 1988 and recently has been restricted to special duties and private hire work only. For this reason it is fitted with an RMC differential which gives the bus quite a surprising turn of speed!

Another interesting vehicle in the Clydeside fleet is RM2083. This bus was originally a Kelvin operated example and was purchased by Clydeside (along with nine others) when Kelvin undertook a fleet reduction in summer 1987. Internally 2083 has been fitted with new flooring, concealed fluorescent lighting and moquette covered seat backs, window surrounds and ceilings. This vehicle has been dubbed the 'Clydemaster' and carries a personal style radiator badge bearing this inscription. Allocated to Johnstone Depot, RM2083 can usually be found on routes 36, 38 or 39.

The 1988 Glasgow Garden Festival saw the Clydeside RM fleet increase by six as additional vehicles were needed for a Festival contract service. These six RMs were used to cover crew operated OPO fitted buses on routes 23 and 24 whilst the OPO vehicles were used on the contract. Three of these RMs (187, 666 and 1032) operated in full Clydeside livery, whilst the other three were finished in all over red with a yellow waistband reminiscent of the recent (and shortlived) London tourist bus livery. All six of these buses are temporarily in store.

It was perhaps the additions to the fleet in February 1988 that put Clydeside one above all other provincial Routemaster operators. Along with five standard RMs (all of which have been broken up for spares) came three RMAs and . . .RML900!

The start of the Clydeside Scottish Routemaster story. RM652 is seen in Paisley undergoing service trials from Johnstone Garage on route 638. During August 1985 RM652 was purchased by Clydeside and as a result was the forerunner of a fleet comprising over 70 Routemaster varients. *(Mike Harris)*

The RML had been withdrawn some months previously by London Buses after sustaining severe frontal accident damage. London Buses had deemed it to be beyond economic repair and had consigned it to the vehicle dump at the former AEC site at Southall. Rumours had been circulating amongst the enthusiast fraternity for some time as to the bus's possible fate and a chance sighting of it being towed through West London by a Clydeside Scottish towing lorry confirmed what everyone had thought. Beyond economic repair in London maybe, but the labour market is very different in Scotland, and using parts from withdrawn RM1984, RML900 was given the full Clydemaster treatment. Advertising space was taken up by the Glasgow *Sunday Post*, the bus being adopted as 'Oor Wullie's Special', Oor Wullie being a well known cartoon character that features in the *Post's* pages. Most surprising was RML900's service debut—in London! Clydeside had entered the RML in the 1988 North Weald Bus Rally on Sunday 19 June and arrangements were made for it to operate in London service the previous day on routes 13 (a.m.) and 26 (p.m.), following the operation of the Finchley Garage showbus RML903 from Clydeside's Thornliebank Depot the previous autumn.

Of the three RMAs, two (RMA29 and 60) are to be used to effect replacement of Bristol Lodekkas on driver training duties, whilst the third (RMA16) is being returned to service condition. This has entailed the fitment of a standard Routemaster three piece destination screen, extensive internal refurbishment à la RM2083 and RML900 with the added refinement of coach seats, and the application of Clydeside's local express coach livery of white and silver. It is intended to allocate this vehicle to Thornliebank Depot on completion of the renovation work which is being carried out at Johnstone. On completion the bus will be classified SRMA1, and be primarily used for private hire and promotional work.

Since RM652 was purchased in October 1985 Clydeside have built up a fleet of over 70 serviceable Routemasters, with many more purchased and dismantled to provide spare parts for the operational fleet. Clydeside Scottish is now the largest operator of RM family vehicles outside London and are committed and enthusiastic Routemaster operators. Recent additions to the fleet and refurbishment work carried out on earlier examples proves the point. The recent purchase of RML900 and its subsequent re-entry into service must surely be the high point of the Clydeside Routemaster story to date.

Clydeside services which see scheduled Routemaster operation

1: Glasgow–Clarkston–Eaglesham
(Mon.–Fri. a.m. peak journeys only)

2: Glasgow–Clarkston–Newton Mearns
(one Mon.–Fri. a.m. peak journey and
one Sat. p.m. journey only)

7: Glasgow–Giffnock–Mearnskirk Hospital
(one Mon.–Fri. p.m. peak journey only)

10: Balornock East–Balornock–Glasgow–Darnley–Pollok
(Mon.–Sat., not evenings, one Sat. p.m. journey
bifacates from Darnley to Neilston)

11: Balornock East–Barmulloch–Glasgow–
Carnwandic/Arden
(Mon.–Sat., not evenings)

17: Howood–Johnstone–Paisley–Clyde Tunnel–Glasgow
(one Mon.–Fri. a.m. peak journey only)

20: Kilmacolm–Johnstone–Paisley
(one Mon.–Fri. a.m. peak journey only)

21: Renfrew Ferry–Paisley–Fairway Avenue
(Mon.–Sat., not evenings)

22: Erskine Hospital–Renfrew–Paisley–Nethercraigs
(Sat. a.m. journeys only)

23: Erskine Hospital–Renfrew–Govan–Glasgow
(40–50% of Mon.–Sat. service RM operated,
not evenings)

24: Nethercraigs–Paisley–Renfrew–Govan–Glasgow
(40–50% of Mon.–Sat. service RM operated,
not evenings)

36: Glasgow–Paisley–Johnstone–Kilbarchan
(Mon.–Sat., not evenings, one a.m. journey
commences from Kilmacolm, one p.m. journey
extends to Brookside)

37: Paisley–Johnstone–Milliken Park
(one Mon.–Fri. a.m. peak journey, return journey
of route 20 listed above)

38: Glasgow–Paisley–Johnstone Castle–Spateston
(Mon.–Sat., not evenings)

39: Glasgow–Paisley–Johnstone–Spateston
(Mon.–Sat., not evenings)

74: Darnley–Eastwood Toll
(one a.m. peak journey only)

81: Renfrew Ferry–Paisley–Foxbar–Paisley
(Sat. early evening journeys only)

84: Glasgow–Govan–Renfrew–Paisley–Nethercraigs–
Foxbar–Paisley
(one Sat. early evening journey only)

93: Kilbarchan–Johnstone High School
(one a.m. peak journey only)

97: Glenpatrick Works–Spateston
(two p.m. peak journeys only)

Clydeside's RML has a designated vehicle running on routes 38 and 39 on Mon.–Fri., viz:

Route 38: Ex Spateston 08.14, 10.47, 13.17, 15.47
Route 39: Ex Glasgow   09.31, 12.01, 14.31, 17.01

On Saturdays the vehicle is officially spare although it does see service as available on routes 36, 38 or 39.

All Clydeside Routemasters are in their depots by approx. 20.00 hrs. The services being driver only operated throughout the evenings and on Sundays.

Initially all Clydeside routes were numbered in the 600 series and very nice they looked too on the newly acquired Routemasters. Sporting a full set of London style blinds, an endearing feature of the Clydeside operation, is RM37 arriving at Paisley on route 613. Subsequently this service has been incorporated into a new route numbered 21. *(Steve Fennell)*

RM1890 stands at Paisley Fereneze Drive on route 622. Note the running number 'I 262'. Although 'I' indicates that the bus is Inchinnan-based, the number 262 is in fact the vehicle's fleet-number. This method of identification was later abandoned, former RM bonnet numbers being retained. *(Steve Fennell)*

Clydeside Scottish Routemaster Fleetlist

Fleet Number	Registration Number	Allocation	Fleet Number	Registration Number	Allocation
RM17§	VLT17	M	RM720†	WLT720	J
RM37	VLT37	J	RM727	WLT727	M
RM48*	VLT48	M	RM794	WLT794	M
RM54*	VLT54	M	RM830	WLT830	M
RM73†	VLT73	J	RM835*	WLT835	M
RM81*	VLT81	J	RM859	WLT859	M
RM104*	VLT104	M	RM870‡	WLT870	M
RM110	VLT110	P	RM874	WLT874	J
RM114	VLT114	J	RM919	WLT919	M
RM154*	VLT154	J	RM924	WLT924	M
RM166	VLT166	J	RM933	WLT933	M
RM187*	VLT187	R	RM936	WLT936	M
RM204	VLT204	M	RM951	WLT951	M
RM206	VLT206	J	RM956*	WLT956	J
RM219	VLT219	M	RM960	WLT960	J
RM226	VLT226	M	RM974	WLT974	J
RM234	VLT234	J	RM978	WLT978	I
RM245	VLT245	M	RM1013	13CLT	M
RM272*	VLT272	J	RM1032	32CLT	R
RM291	VLT291	I	RM1054	54CLT	M
RM303	WLT303	M	RM1134	134CLT	M
RM305	WLT305	J	RM1152	152CLT	P
RM364	WLT364	J	RM1267	267CLT	J
RM367	WLT367	J	RM1703«	703DYE	R
RM391*	WLT391	J	RM1731«	731DYE	R
RM416	WLT416	M	RM1803	803DYE	M
RM441*	WLT441	J	RM1890	ALD890B	I
RM444	WLT444	I	RM1913	ALD913B	P
RM447	WLT447	M	RM1959	ALD959B	P
RM465	WLT465	P	RM2048	ALM48B	M
RM495	WLT495	J	RM2083c	ALM83B	J
RM501	WLT501	J	RM2107‡	CUV107C	M
RM526	WLT526	J	RM2208«	CUV208C	R
RM546	WLT546	I	RM2210	CUV210C	P
RM550	WLT550	J	RML900**	WLT900	J
RM641*	WLT641	M			
RM652	WLT652	P	RMA29	KGJ603D	–
RM666	WLT666	R	RMA60	NMY658E	–
RM694°	WLT694	P			
RM697	WLT697	M	SRMA1 (RMA16)	KGJ614D	M

Allocation codes: I=Inchinnan   J=Johnstone   M=Thornliebank   P=Paisley   R=Reserve fleet, unallocated

* Indicates that bus carries early body with non opening front upper deck windows.

† Indicates that bus carries early body with non opening front upper deck windows but is temporarily fitted with one opener and one non opener.

§ Bus carries overall advertisement livery for Westcars (a local motor dealer).

° Bus carries wrap around advertisement for Balfour Beatty.

‡ Bus is fitted with Leyland engine.

« Bus is painted all over red livery with yellow waistband.

c The Clydemaster. Bus fitted with fluorescent lighting, wall to wall moquette, new flooring and heating.

** Bus carries wrap around advertisement for the *Sunday Post* local paper. Interior finished to similar style to that carried by RM2083 (c above).

RMs 28, 33, 162, 233, 265, 473, 588, 724, 847, 878, 1261, 1308, 1407, 1565, 1587, 1625, 1667, 1705, 1768, 1830, 1915, 1916, 1984, 1987, 2053, 2095, 2096 and 2203 were acquired for spare parts only. RM473 subsequently passed to Strathtay Scottish.

RMs 187, 447, 666, 936, 978, 1032, 1803 and 2107 were acquired from Scottish Bus Group Engineering and placed in the operational fleet. RMs 1959 and 2083 were acquired from Kelvin Scottish and similarly placed in the operational fleet.

RMs 983, 984, 2006, 2058, 2086, 2102, 2108 and 2115 were also acquired from Kelvin Scottish but broken up for spare parts.

RM200 was acquired from Scottish Bus Group Engineering, it is thought that this bus will also be used as a source of spare parts.

Many of those RMs listed above as acquired for spare parts are still intact and it could well be that some of these might be placed into service, possibly as a replacement for some less healthy examples.

The successor for the 613, illustrated earlier, was the 21. RM444 is seen in Paisley heading for the northen terminus of Renfrew Ferry. The short ferry crossing over the Clyde brings one to Kelvin Scottish Routemaster operations on routes 5 and 5A. *(Steve Fennell)*

Inchinnan Depot's entire Routemaster allocation is specially posed at the Depot on Sunday 24 April 1988. The use of an RM on route 25 was notable. One Saturday evening trip as far as Bishopton was sometimes RM operated. RM978, nearest the camera, had in fact performed the journey the previous evening. This working has since been withdrawn. *(Steve Fennell)*

RM1152 stands at Paisley Nethercraigs after working a Saturday morning crew journey on route 22. This bus will now work on to the 24 upon which it will remain for the remainder of the day. Route 22's normal allocation being driver only operated buses. *(Steve Fennell)*

Still carrying the advert frame applied by London Buses, RM2210 is a fairly late addition to the Clydeside fleet. Seen here at Govan Underground Station on route 24. *(Steve Fennell)*

Johnstone Depot are responsible for providing the trunk service along the Paisley Road into Glasgow. Seen waiting time in Paisley is **RM234** sporting a somewhat large dent in its front roofdome. *(Steve Fennell)*

RM720 is one of two Clydeside Routemasters that have been temporarily fitted with the 'wrong' type of front window following accident damage. Note the front upper deck windows. The 'opener' will be replaced as soon as a plain frame can be obtained. *(Steve Fennell)*

A grim April day at the Balornock East Terminus of routes 10 and 11 finds four RMs in evidence on this high frequency service. RM305 has just arrived whilst the stand is occupied by RMs 48, 936 and 951. *(Steve Fennell)*

Glasgow Buchanan Street Bus Station plays host to RM2107 performing an unscheduled working on the 1, whilst alongside is RM546 on private hire and Plaxton bodied Tiger P478. Note that the coach carries a former Routemaster registration transferred from a scrap vehicle. RM2107 incidentally is only one of two Clydeside Routemasters to be fitted with Leyland engines. *(Steve Fennell)*

A particularly interesting Routemaster in the Clydeside fleet is RM2083 which has been extensively renovated internally. It is seen here at Kilmacolm on the morning Routemaster journey on route 20. *(Steve Fennell)*

Internally, new flooring, moquette trim and fluorescent lighting have all been installed as well as a continuous bell push along the length of the upper saloon. The traditional bellcord being retained on the lower level! Illustrated is the renovated upper deck, the fluorescent lights being concealed behind the advertisement panels, clearly seen here. *(Steve Fennell)*

RM2083 has been christened the 'Clydemaster' and carries a special blue triangle incorporating not only its parentage but also its new name! *(Steve Fennell)*

With such a large Routemaster fleet it is perhaps inevitable that livery variations will occur. Seen at Thornliebank Depot are RMs 526 and 697, both prior to entering service. RM697 carries an experimental variation of Clydeside colours incorporating a large yellow wedge front. Fortunately this particular scheme was firmly rejected and the bus was repainted into the more traditional styling as seen on RM526 before entering service. *(Steve Fennell)*

RM416 received a 'half-n-half' Clydeside/London livery scheme to promote the Aberlour Children in Need Appeal, although the vehicle was repainted in normal fleet colours in April 1988. Clearly displaying this most unusual livery, RM416 is seen at Ayr making a special appearance on route 4. *(John Burnett)*

RM694 currently carries a 'wrap-around' scheme for Balfour Beatty. The bus is seen at Paisley Nethercraigs on the evening Routemaster journey on route 84. *(Steve Fennell)*

Six additional Routemasters were prepared for service during spring 1988 so as indirectly provide a pool of spare vehicles to enable the company to undertake the provision of a special service in conjunction with the 1988 Glasgow Garden Festival. Three of these buses were finished in an allover red livery with yellow waistband similar to the short-lived London Tourist Bus scheme. RM2208 is posed at Johnstone Depot during April 1988 carrying a set of Thornliebank destination blinds. At the time of writing these three RMs are all in store albeit retaining this livery. However, repainting in full Clydeside colours is expected shortly as these buses are intended to implement a slight expansion of crew operation in the very near future. *(Steve Fennell)*

The only overall advertisement Routemaster in the Clydeside fleet is RM17, carrying a white and blue colour scheme promoting 'Westcars', a local SAAB dealer. Allocated to Thornliebank Depot, RM17 is seen here at the Balornock East terminus of route 11. *(Steve Fennell)*

Perhaps the most well known Clydeside Routemaster is RML900, obtained by Clydeside in accident damaged condition in February 1988. Following a rather extensive repair job aided no doubt by the take-up of the advertising space by the local Glasgow Sunday paper, RML900 returned to service in June 1988. Internally, the bus has been given the full 'RM2083' treatment (see page 17) and has been fitted with a non opening driver's windscreen and 'DMS style' trafficators. These later modifications will be incorporated on other Clydeside Routemasters as and when required. RML900's service debut was in London on Saturday 18 June, the day prior to the annual North Weald Rally in which the bus had been entered. In pristine condition, RML900 is seen in New Barnet on LT route 26. *(Steve Fennell)*

The latest addition to the Clydeside Routemaster fleet is the newly reclassified SRMA1, formally RMA16. Finished in 'quicksilver' livery of white and silver, the unique vehicle is seen at Johnstone Depot in October 1988. At the time of photography the interior renovation had still to be completed. *(Steve Fennell)*

Kelvin Scottish Omnibus Co. Ltd

During August 1985 Kelvin Scottish borrowed Clydeside's RM652 and evaluated it from their Kirkintilloch Depot for two days. On its return to Clydeside no decision was taken immediately and it was not until November that a further two Clydeside examples were taken on loan for further trials. These trials lasted almost six weeks and soon after their completion an announcement was made that a total of 59 Routemasters were to be obtained for service. The first bus to be taken into stock was RM371, being received from London Buses in February 1986. Initially the first Routemasters to be obtained were prepared for service by the now closed London Transport Aldenham Bus Overhaul Works but later acquisitions were prepared by Scottish Bus Group Engineering at Kilmarnock.

Kelvin placed RM371 directly into store upon its arrival, preferring to wait until sufficient buses were in stock to enable a full route conversion to take place. However, 371 became the first Kelvin example to carry fare paying passengers when it was loaned to Clydeside Scottish on the occasion of that company's Greenock Depot Open Day on 22 March 1986 when it made its service debut on various Greenock local services. After these exertions the bus returned to store and it was not until June of the same year that sufficient RMs had been delivered to enable the conversion of routes 300 and 301 to crew operation to take place. Route 300 was a peak hour express service running from Glasgow to Easterhouse, whilst the 301 operated from Glasgow to Bridgeton Cross via Easterhouse. Initially, the RMs were out in service until last bus at night but later service changes slightly curtailed their hours of operation! Both the 300 and 301 were operated from the company's Stepps Depot.

Throughout the summer Kelvin's stock of Routemasters was gradually increased in preparation for 'D Day' in October 1986; in fact it was in advance of this historic date that the next batch of RMs entered service. From 1 September 1986 almost 40 Routemasters were introduced to new routes 5 and 5A, giving rise to allocations at Old Kilpatrick and Milngavie Depots. Coincidental with the introduction of these services was the withdrawal of routes 300 and 301, the RMs transferring to the new operations on the 5 and 5A. These two services combined to provide a joint five minute headway across Glasgow City Centre from Easterhouse in the east to Faifley and Old Kilpatrick in the west. Further Routemasters entered service from 'D Day' itself when route 6 was introduced. This service ran, once again, from Easterhouse across the City Centre to Pollok and was a direct attack against the services of Strathclyde's Buses, since becoming a self-autonomous company without PTE involvement. In all events the 6 was not entirely successful as the Routemasters were removed from the service the following January and introduced instead on to route 61, another cross City service linking Summerston with Baillieston.

During early 1987, Kelvin started experiencing serious vehicle problems with consequent effects on service reliability. In order to assist in alleviating this problem various buses were hired in from other companies. Included in these vehicles were two Routemasters from Strathtay Scottish. These two RMs (26 and 191) had yet to see service with Strathtay and, in fact, were not to do so until June the same year. In the meantime, they were allocated to Milngavie Depot and were used extensively on routes 5 and 5A. This vehicle shortage was the least of Kelvin's problems however as it became evident that the financial returns on this ambitious expansion of services was not all it should be! A direct result of the company's worsening financial position was the imposition of a rather savage round of service reductions and withdrawals from 12th July 1987. The upshot of all this in terms of the Routemaster fleet was a reduction in fleet strength to only 40 examples. The economies which threw up this substantial Routemaster reduction was the withdrawal of part of route 61 (the Glasgow–Summerston section) and a frequency reduction on routes 5 and 5A. At the same time the Baillieston section of route 61 was converted to OPO. Even this drastic course of action was insufficient to stem the tide and, from October, the depot at Milngavie was closed, concentrating the remaining Routemasters at Stepps and Old Kilpatrick.

Initially identification of the Kelvin Routemasters was made easy by virtue of the fact that the existing RM bonnet number was retained along with the London registration number. Kelvin's intention was to wait until all RMs were in stock and then renumber the fleet from 1901 upwards in chronological order. However, by the time this plan was instigated the Routemaster fleet total had been reduced to 40 buses and some were never to carry their intended fleet number. The fleet renumbering commenced during summer 1987 and at the same time the practice of re-registering Routemasters with 'A suffix' marks commenced. The original RM registrations were either sold or in some cases transferred to coaches in the Kelvin fleet. All Routemasters which originally carried non-suffix marks have now been re-registered which, along with the new fleet numbers, makes initial identification of individual buses somewhat difficult!

The present Kelvin RM situation sees only routes 5 and 5A worked by this type. In common with most other operators only the Mon.–Sat. daytime service is crew worked; at other times the service is provided by driver only operated vehicles. A small number of peak hour RM workings still remain on the truncated 61 route whilst a particularly interesting operation, which has only recently ceased, was the provision of two RM journeys on Strathclyde PTE subsidised service 168 which operated from Clydebank to Erskine via the Erskine Bridge. Both of these journeys were through buses from Easterhouse on route 5 and this route number was shown on the majority of occasions. 168, in fact, not being incorporated on Kelvin's Routemaster blinds.

Of the RMs withdrawn in July 1987, ten examples passed to Clydeside Scottish, two for further service and the balance for spare parts, whilst six buses passed to the Stagecoach Group and are now part of the Cumberland Motor Services fleet based in Carlisle. The outstanding balance of these vehicles went for scrap.

5: Easterhouse–Dennistoun–Glasgow City Centre–
Clydebank–Old Kilpatrick
(Mon.–Sat., not evenings)

5A: Easterhouse–Springboig–Glasgow City Centre–
Clydebank–Faifley
(Mon.–Sat., not evenings)

61: Glasgow City Centre–Baillieston
(one a.m. peak and one p.m. peak
Mon.–Fri. journey only)

RMs 716, 922, 976, 2027, 2045 and 2056 were acquired for spare parts only.

The following RMs were deleted from stock in July 1987:
250, 280, 293, 605, 706, 824, 875, 983, 984, 1933, 1941, 1959, 1983, 2006, 2035, 2058, 2070, 2072, 2073, 2083, 2086, 2102, 2108 and 2115.

RMs 2035 and 2073 were subsequently reinstated whilst RMs 983, 984, 1959, 2006, 2058, 2083, 2086, 2102, 2108 and 2115 passed to Clydeside Scottish, 1959 and 2083 for further service. The balance for spare parts.

RMs 706, 824, 875, 1933, 1941 and 1983 were sold to the Stagecoach Group for use in the Cumberland Motor Services fleet. The remainder were sold for scrap.

* Indicates the bus carries early body with non opening upper deck front windows. Kelvin 1922 (RM741) has, following accident damage, been fitted with one opening window alongside the non opening example (see page 23).

Allocation codes: OK=Old Kilpatrick   SS=Stepps

Kelvin Scottish Routemaster Fleetlist

Kelvin Fleet No.	RM No.	Current Registration Number	Original Registration Number	Depot Allocation
1901*	RM22	EDS111A	VLT22	SS
1902*	RM55	EDS128A	VLT55	SS
1903	RM149	EDS117A	VLT149	SS
1904	RM177	EDS130A	VLT177	SS
1905	RM229	EDS134A	VLT229	SS
1906	RM288	EDS125A	VLT288	SS
1907	RM290	EDS120A	VLT290	OK
1908	RM321	YTS824A	WLT321	OK
1909	RM357	EDS278A	WLT357	OK
1910	RM371	EDS281A	WLT371	OK
1911*	RM388	EDS300A	WLT388	SS
1912	RM408	EDS282A	WLT408	SS
1913	RM415	EDS285A	WLT415	SS
1914	RM419	EDS393A	WLT419	SS
1915	RM439	EDS392A	WLT439	SS
1916	RM471	EDS394A	WLT471	SS
1917	RM480	EDS381A	WLT480	SS
1918	RM538	EDS395A	WLT538	SS
1919*	RM606	EDS320A	WLT606	OK
1920*	RM677	WTS164A	WLT677	OK
1921	RM678	EDS293A	WLT678	OK
1922*	RM741	EDS295A	WLT741	OK
1923*	RM774	EDS397A	WLT774	OK
1924*	RM760	EDS297A	WLT760	OK
1925	RM770	EDS277A	WLT770	SS
1926	RM799	EDS312A	WLT799	OK
1927	RM809	EDS396A	WLT809	OK
1928	RM858	EDS362A	WLT858	OK
1929	RM910	EDS288A	WLT910	OK
1930	RM915	EDS401A	WLT915	OK
1931	RM987	EDS352A	WLT987	OK
1932	RM1006	EDS98A	6CLT	OK
1933	RM1010	EDS221A	10CLT	OK
1934	RM1040	EDS109A	40CLT	OK
1935	RM1053	EDS107A	53CLT	OK
1936	RM1149	WTS163A	149CLT	OK
1937	RM1630	EDS537B	630DYE	OK
1938	RM2081	ALM81B	–	SS
1939	RM2073	ALM73B	–	SS
1940	RM2035	ALM35B	–	OK

Facing page: **Kelvin Scottish's first Routemasters entered service in June 1986 on routes 300 and 301. These operations were particularly shortlived and both services were withdrawn from the following September. RM1040 is seen arriving at Buchanan Street Bus Station Glasgow in July 1986. At this stage the habit of reregistering vehicles with non-suffix marks had yet to be thought of!** *(Steve Fennell)*

This page top: **Following the withdrawal of approximately 20 Routemasters in summer 1987, a number were retained by Kelvin and broken up for spare parts. Such was the fate of RMs 250 and 2070, seen here at Old Kilpatrick Depot in April 1988.** *(Steve Fennell)*

This page middle: **Kelvin 1922 alias RM741 is seen at Old Kilpatrick carrying an opening front upper deck window in place of the plain variety following accident damage.** *(Steve Fennell)*

This page bottom: **January 1987 saw the allocation of Routemasters to route 61, although their use on this service was to last only a little under six months. RM2035 is seen in Bailieston on the last day of crew operation, 11 July 1987.** *(Philip Hanwell)*

By September 1988 all of Kelvin's Routemasters with non-suffix registrations had been re-registered with the more valuable non-suffix marks being either sold or transferred to other company vehicles. Such is the case on Kelvin 4319, a Duple bodied Leyland Tiger seen at Crianlarich bearing RM678's former registration. *(Steve Fennell)*

Meanwhile, the real RM678 carries EDS293A. Along with its new fleetnumber (1921), initial identification of the bus is extremely difficult. RM678 is seen at Clydebank. *(Steve Fennell)*

Top:
Kelvin 1932 (RM1006) and 1933 (RM1010) are seen at the Yoker Ferry. Approximately half a mile away is the terminus of Clydeside's RM route 21 on the south bank of the Clyde. *(Steve Fennell)*

Middle:
Kelvin 1937 (RM1630) waits time at Clydebank Station. When first acquired by Kelvin and during the period when RM numbers were retained this bus was inadvertently christened RM630.
(Steve Fennell)

Bottom:
Kelvin 1906 (RM288) arrives at Clydebank Bus Stance on a journey to Easterhouse. Note that two different liveries are carried by Kelvin's Routemasters. The horizontal lines on the side panels being lower on this particular bus than on some vehicles previously illustrated: the buses carrying the 'lower' style of livery being Kelvin's earlier acquisitions. Since the Routemasters were purchased a much simpler version of livery has been introduced by Kelvin, albeit still retaining the same colours. Whether any RMs receive this later style of livery remains to be seen.
(Steve Fennell)

Strathtay Scottish Omnibus Co. Ltd

Following the loan of Clydeside Scottish RMs 219 and 272 which were evaluated in Dundee and Perth late in 1985, Strathtay Scottish acquired 20 RMs for service commencing with RM42 which was delivered in spring 1986. Ad hoc operation of Routemasters occurred in both Dundee and Perth prior to 'D Day' in October 1986 when full RM allocations were made at both Dundee and Perth. At Dundee nine RMs were allocated where they took over the bulk of the service on routes 75, 76 and 77 between Carnoustie/Monifieth, Dundee City Centre and Ninewalls Hospital/Wormit. Perth Depot was allocated the balance of 11 buses which were employed on routes 1 and 2 (Perth City Centre, Letham/Tulloch circulars) and route 3 (City Centre–North Muirton).

The Dundee services took the Routemasters over the Tay Road Bridge on what was perhaps the most spectacular RM ride in the country whilst undertaking the Wormit section of route. Furthermore, one Saturday evening journey was extended on from Wormit to Gauldry, this section of route being rural in the extreme! Regrettably, from February 1988 the crew resources at Dundee were restructured and RMs no longer cross the Tay to Wormit or Gauldry on a scheduled basis. The whole crew service being restricted to the north side of the Tay.

The livery of the original Strathtay batch was a very striking blue, orange and white colour scheme. London style destination blinds were supplied apart from the route number blinds at Perth which were produced locally. Rear blinds were not fitted and the relevant apertures were painted over.

In March 1987 two further Routemasters were obtained for service and these were painted in a far more traditional style of livery albeit retaining the same blue, orange and white colours. However, at that time Kelvin Scottish were experiencing a chronic shortage of serviceable vehicles and these two buses were immediately loaned to Kelvin without seeing service in their native Strathtay area. Both were allocated to Milngavie Depot and ran alongside their Kelvin cousins primarily on routes 5 and 5A. During the early summer both of these rogue RMs were sent on to their rightful owners and after a short while were allocated to Arbroath Depot for use on routes 73 and 74 between Arbroath/Carnoustie, Dundee and Invergowrie. This particular operation was somewhat shortlived however as the buses themselves were inadequate to cater for the traffic on offer and they were replaced by fleetlines, which retained conductors. The two redundant RMs were then allocated to Dundee Depot where they were used to boost the existing allocation. Strathtay started re-registering their Routemasters from August 1987 and transferring the 'dateless' RM registrations to coaches within their fleet. At the time of writing only a handful of RMs remain with their original numbers thus making initial identification of these vehicles somewhat difficult.

During March/April 1988 a further five RMs were obtained and three of these were prepared for service. This gave Strathtay some spare RMs and as a result various loans were made to other companies who wished to evaluate the potential of a Routemaster. SR1 (RM943) was loaned to Northern General in March 1988 where it was evaluated, along with a further privately owned example, on routes radiating from Newcastle and Gateshead. This loan lasted only two weeks before the vehicle was returned to Dundee. The irony of this situation should not be overlooked. In earlier years, Northern General operated a quite sizeable fleet of Routemasters and were, in fact, the only customer outside London to purchase such vehicles new, albeit the front entrance version which never found much favour in London! Other loans have been to Highland Scottish and at the time of writing two RMs are to be found in Inverness fighting it out on the streets with the newly formed 'Inverness Traction Company'. Whether Highland eventually purchase Routemasters of their own in an attempt to ward off this competitor remains to be seen. During summer 1988 SR20 (RM917) was repainted and was outshopped in the livery style applied to SRs 21–25. It is assumed that all future repaints will be to this pattern.

**Strathtay services
which see scheduled Routemaster operation**

1: Perth City Centre–Letham–Tulloch–Perth City Centre
(Mon.–Sat., not evenings)

2: Perth City Centre–Tulloch–Letham–Perth City Centre
(Mon.–Sat., not evenings)

3: Perth City Centre–North Muirton
(Mon.–Sat., not evenings)

11: Perth City Centre–Kinnoull Hill–Perth City Centre
(one Mon.–Fri a.m. journey only)

73: Dundee City Centre–Broughty Ferry–
Monifieth Ashludie Hospital
(one Mon.–Sat. early a.m. journey only)

74: Dundee City Centre–Broughty Ferry–Monifieth–
Carnoustie
(one Mon.–Fri. p.m. peak journey only)

75: Carnoustie (peak hours)–Monifieth Ashludie Hospital/
Ashludie Terrace/Broomhill Drive–Broughty Ferry–
Dundee City Centre–Perth Road–Ninewells Hospital.
Some journeys operate via Strathern Road between
Dundee and Monifieth
(Mon.–Sat., not evenings)

76: Carnoustie (peak hours)–Monifieth Ashludie Hospital/
Ashludie Terrace/Broomhill Drive–Broughty Ferry–
Dundee City Centre–Perth Road–Kingoodie
(Mon.–Sat., not evenings)

Strathtay Scottish Routemaster Fleetlist

Strathtay Fleet No.	RM No.	Registration Number	Original Registration Number	Depot Allocation
SR1	RM943	WTS225A	WLT943	D
SR2*	RM298	WTS245A	VLT298	D
SR3	RM759	WTS329A	WLT759	D
SR4	RM1017	YTS973A	17CLT	D
SR5	RM702	WLT702	–	D
SR6	RM1821	YLS32B	821DYE	D
SR7	RM1691	WYS87A	691DYE	D
SR8	RM921	YTS892A	WLT921	D
SR9*	RM217	WTS131A	VLT217	D
SR10	RM427	YTS867A	WLT427	P
SR11	RM743	WTS268A	WLT743	P
SR12	RM183	WTS101A	VLT183	P
SR13*	RM42	WTS97A	VLT42	P
SR14	RM1911	ALD911B	–	P
SR15	RM1874	ALD874B	–	P
SR16	RM610	WTS316A	WLT610	P
SR17*	RM93	WTS109A	VLT93	P
SR18*	RM1914	ALD914B	–	P
SR19	RM221	WTS128A	VLT221	P
SR20	RM917	WTS102A	WLT917	R
SR21	RM26	VLT26	–	D
SR22	RM191	VLT191	–	R
SR23*	RM45	VLT45	–	R
SR24	RM1143	WTS186A	143CLT	P
SR25	RM316	WTS333A	WLT316	P

SRs 5, 22 and 23 are expected to lose their London registration marks in the very near future.

RMs 38, 473, 588, 680, 699, 784, 1048 and 1300 were also acquired for spare parts only. RM588 has subsequently passed to Clydeside Scottish for the same purpose.

Allocation codes:
D=Dundee   P=Perth   R=Reserve fleet, unallocated

* Indicates that bus carries early body with non opening upper deck front windows. SR18 (RM1914) is particularly noteworthy as it is unusual for such a high stock number to carry such a body, in this case body B22. The former London Transport overhaul system of body changing usually managed to avoid such anomalies.

Early Strathtay Routemaster operation saw their use on route 77 which crosses the Tay Road Bridge. SR2 (RM298) waits in Dundee on a gloomy day in November 1986. *(Steve Fennell)*

This page top:
SR7 (RM1691) is seen on route 76 in Dundee City Centre. Following the February 1988 route restructuring these short workings between the City and Monifieth were renumbered 75, the 76 number being used instead for the through service to Invergowrie and Kingoodie. *(Steve Fennell)*

This page bottom:
Monifieth Ashludie Hospital terminus sees SR8 (RM921) carrying its new registration number YTS892A. It is intended that all Strathtay RMs other than those with genuine London 'B' suffix marks and SR21 (RM26) will be so treated. The London registrations being transferred to coaches in the Strathtay fleet. *(Steve Fennell)*

Facing page top:
At the time of writing, one evening peak journey on route 74 is operated by a Routemaster. SR5 (RM702) arrives at Dundee City Centre. *(Steve Fennell)*

Facing page middle:
From February 1988 Kingoodie to the south of the City benefited from Routemaster operation. SR3 (RM759) is seen at Kingoodie terminus in April 1988. *(Steve Fennell)*

Facing page bottom:
SR2 (RM298) now carries WTS245A instead of its traditional VLT298. Seen outside Dundee Bus Station in September 1988. *(Steve Fennell)*

Strathtay Scottish

Strathtay obtained two further RMs in March 1987 and these were painted in a much more restrained style of Strathtay's livery. It is expected that this scheme will be adopted for the whole RM fleet once repaints become due. SR21 (RM26) is seen at Wormit in April 1988 making an unscheduled appearance on route 77. *(Steve Fennell)*

Three further RMs were acquired for service early in 1988 and these three were all finished in the later style of livery and allocated to the reserve fleet. One of these buses was RM45, best remembered for being the former LT Radio Training Bus and as a result not having seen passenger service for some years. Two Strathtay Routemasters are currently on loan to Highland Scottish for use in Inverness and one of the vehicles there is RM45. The use of Highland's Routemasters is somewhat irregular and on Monday 5 September both SRs 22 and 23 (RMs 191 and 45 respectively) were to be found out of use in Inverness Depot. Fortunately with the help of co-operative depot staff this photograph was obtained. *(Steve Fennell)*

Perth's Routemasters all operate on short City services, two of which are circular around the Letham and Tulloch areas. SR17 (RM93) commences its journey around the Letham/Tulloch loop and is seen in Perth City Centre.
(Russell Upcraft)

The latest addition to the Strathtay Routemaster fleet is RM316. Now numbered SR25 and re-registered with a non-London mark the bus is seen on route 2 in Perth. This is the only Strathtay Routemaster to retain the advertisement frame fitted by London Buses shortly before withdrawal from London service.
(Russell Upcraft)

The other Perth City Service which sees regular Routemaster operation is the 3 which operates from the City Centre to North Muirton. SR13 (RM42) is illustrated at the North Muirton terminus.
(Steve Fennell)

Although all Strathtay Routemasters had destination blinds supplied by London Transport (apart from the route number blinds at Perth which were locally produced) the panel for route 3 was changed shortly after Routemaster operation commenced to this distinctly non-London style display. SR12 (RM183) is seen in Mill Street, Perth. New destination blind sets for Perth are currently being delivered and these are very similar in style to those produced by London. *(Steve Fennell)*

One morning journey is Routemaster operated on route 11 from Perth to Kinnoull Hill and return. SR13 (RM42) waits for departure time in South Street, Perth. *(Philip Hanwell)*

Mill Street, Perth plays host to SR11 (RM743) making a most unusual appearance on route 5. Overtaking is SR24 (RM1143) one of Strathtay's latest acquisitions on the more usual service 2. It is believed that roadworks had precluded the 5 from operating over its through route and that this bus was merely providing a shuttle service over one section. *(Philip Hanwell)*

Facing page top:
Verwood Transport's RMA11 is seen at Poole displaying the very smart two-tone blue livery adopted for two of the company's Routemasters. Most unusually the vehicle is operated as an OPO bus. *(Steve Fennell)*

Facing page middle:
Early days of Southampton City-Bus Routemaster operation are represented by Southampton 405 (RM1363). This bus has since been withdrawn. *(Steve Fennell)*

Facing page bottom:
Magicbus RM1741 is seen at Buchanan Bus Station Glasgow on the Easterhouse service. This livery is to be adopted for the Cumberland Motor Services and United Counties fleets. This particular bus has since been sold to David Coster of Hull and is illustrated again under new ownership on page 64. *(Steve Fennell)*

FLASH
GORDON
FILMS
Tel: 826724
POOLE DIRECT
102
RMA 11
VERWOOD TRANSPORT
NMY 648 E

MARKS
Perrings
THE BEST WAY BETWEEN MILLBROOK, SHIRLEY AND THE CITY
HOP
ON
AT
THE
BACK
16
Station
Shirley
Redbridge Hill
Millbrook Est.
16
16
SOUTHAMPTON
CityBus
405
YOUR CARD
363 CLT

19 EXPRESS
EASTERHOUSE CIRCULAR
MAGICBUS
magicbus
741 DYE

Cumberland Motor Services 903 (RM1983) approaches Carlisle City Centre on route 61. *(Steve Fennell)*

Kelvin Scottish RM419 is seen at Faifley on route 5A. This vehicle has since been allocated a new fleet number, 1914, and re-registered EDS393A. *(Steve Fennell)*

Strathtay Scottish SR18 (RM1914) is seen at the North Muirton terminus on route 3. Note that the bus carries an early body with non opening upper deck front windows, unusual for such a high stock number. *(Steve Fennell)*

UCOC702 (RM528) is seen at Putnoe on route 101. *(Steve Fennell)*

Burnley & Pendle
23
EASTENDER
via
Brierfield
& Nelson
Colne
EastEnders
Burnley & Pendle
Army Careers Inform
CUV 114 C

11
Shawlands City Centre
Pollok Road
Barmulloch
CARNWADRIC
Clydeside
SCOTTISH
RM933
Welcome aboard.
We're going your way.
WLT 933

12
BLACKPOOL
TRAVEL
CARD
3 DAYS UNLIMITED TRAVEL ON
BLACKPOOL'S TRAMS & BUSES
Details from
Blackpool
Transport offices
tel 0253 23931
BLACKPOOL TRANSPORT
525
TELEVISION HOUSE
650 DYE

Blackpool Transport Services Ltd

Blackpool Transport (and predecessors) have always recognised the merits of crew operated buses, retaining them long after other operators have discarded them in favour of the economics of the driver only operated version! Indeed, a number of Leyland PD3s still exist in the fleet today, and seem strangely archaic with their manual transmission, almost representative of an age no longer with us. Some would say that with this track record it would only have been a matter of time before surplus London Routemasters would join the fleet and so it was in January 1986 that Leyland engined RM1583 travelled north from London for two weeks' evaluation in this Lancashire town. In fact, RM1583 never returned to London and was purchased, along with three others, in April 1986. Two further buses were acquired the following month, and all were placed into service on routes 5 and 5A (Grange Park–Town Centre–Halfway House) in full London livery with the LT bullseye symbol simply painted over. In common with RM1583, all of these purchases were equipped with Leyland engines. RM1583, meanwhile, had been taken in works for a full repaint into Blackpool colours and it was with considerable surprise that some weeks later it emerged in a superb red and white colour scheme with gold and black lining, Blackpool's present day colours being green and white! In fact, the livery chosen was based on the company's pre-war scheme and all of the initial batch of six Routemasters were finished in this smartly attired livery.

In October 1986 the RMs were transferred on to route 12 which operated from the Town Centre to Squires Gate Airport with a subsequent extension to St Annes. The 12 service is supplemented over the section of route as far as Lindale Gardens, Lytham Road by a frequent service of minibuses. In fact, the whole evening and Sunday service is minibus operated, including the section of route through to St Annes.

It was not until April 1988 that further Routemasters were to join the Blackpool fleet when an additional six buses, all Leyland examples, were purchased. These later acquisitions were intended for a new service running from

Gynn Square along the promenade to Starr Gate. Subsequently numbered 55, the route was provided in response to a predatory strike by Fylde Borough Transport who had commenced operating a 'Baby Blue' minibus service along the promenade in direct competition with the famous tramway. Fylde adopted the route number 55 for their service and christened it the 'Beachcomber'. Blackpool Transport, not to be outdone, chose the same route number and tagged their service the 'Beachroamer'! The passenger seeking transport along the sea-front now has the choice of Trams, Routemasters or Minibuses. From an enthusiast's point of view it is fairly conclusive which one of these options is a non-starter!

The six RMs acquired for the 55 have also been finished in a red and white colour scheme but without the elaborate lining out as on their predecessors. Former RM numbers, as well as Blackpool's own fleet number, are carried and this also applies to the earlier batch. At the time of writing rumours persist that yet further Routemasters are to join the Blackpool fleet. However, the stock of Leyland engined vehicles remaining with London is very low which suggests that purchase will have to be sooner rather than later if this course of action is decided upon.

Blackpool Transport services which see scheduled Routemaster operation

12: Blackpool Town Centre–Lytham Road–Squires Gate–St Annes (Mon.–Sat. not evenings)

55: Gynn Square–North Pier–Tower–Pleasure Beach–Starr Gate (Daily operation, not evenings)

In addition an RM can also be found fairly frequently on the following:

14: Blackpool Town Centre–Layton–Thornton–Fleetwood

22 & 22A: Cleveleys–Bispham–Layton–Blackpool Town Centre–St Annes–Lytham.

Blackpool Transport Routemaster Fleetlist

Blackpool Fleet No.	RM No.	Registration Number
521	RM1583	583CLT
522	RM848	WLT848
523	RM1627	627DYE
524	RM1640	640DYE
525	RM1650	650DYE
526	RM1735	735DYE
527	RM879	WLT879
528	RM1357	357CLT
529	RM1966	ALD966B
530	RM1989	ALD989B
531	RM2071	ALM71B
533	RM2089	ALM89B

Facing page top:
Burnley 184 (RM2114) leaves Burnley on the short journey to Colne. *(Steve Fennell)*

Facing page middle:
Clydeside Scottish RM933 is seen at the Balornock East terminus of the busy 10 and 11 services. Joint headways provide a bus every five minutes during the day. *(Steve Fennell)*

Facing page bottom:
Blackpool 525 (RM1650) is illustrated at the St Anne's alighting point on route 12. *(Steve Fennell)*

Shortly after introduction, Blackpool 524 (RM1640) is seen at Grange Park. The use of Routemasters on routes 5 and 5A lasted only a few months. *(Steve Fennell)*

Since October 1986 the initial batch of Blackpool Routemasters can normally be found on route 12. Illustrated here is Blackpool 522 (RM848) near Central Pier. *(Steve Fennell)*

Just occasionally an RM can be seen operating to Fleetwood on route 14. Fairly common shortly after the Routemasters' arrival, appearances these days are somewhat rarer. Blackpool 521 (RM1583) is seen in August 1986.
(Malcolm King)

During the summer months the frequency on route 12 is increased to provide a bus every 15 minutes through to St Anne's instead of half-hourly. Blackpool 523 (RM1627) pulls out of Lytham Road on its way to St Anne's. *(Steve Fennell)*

Although the daytime allocation on route 12 is intended to be Routemaster operated, Blackpool Transport's venerable Leyland PD3s are certainly no strangers to the service. Blackpool 512, finished in a similar red and white colour scheme to the RMs, leaves Talbot Road Bus Station. Fifteen minutes later Blackpool 524 (RM1640) will follow. *(Steve Fennell)*

The second batch of Routemasters to join the Blackpool fleet do not possess the elaborate style of lining out as on their predecessors. Displaying an incorrect destination, Blackpool 531 (RM2071) heads for Starr Gate on 'Beachroamer' 55. *(Steve Fennell)*

Two forms of transport, both very popular with enthusiasts, vie for custom at Gynn Square. Blackpool 525 (RM1650), one of Blackpool's first batch of Routemasters, is unusually seen on the 55. Note the far more elaborate style of livery prevalent on these earlier acquisitions.
(Steve Fennell)

Blackpool 528 (RM1357) picks up outside the famous Tower. All of Blackpool's RMs are fitted with Leyland engines. *(Steve Fennell)*

Southampton City-Bus

fter the acquisition of 'Hampshire Bus' by the Stagecoach Group in early 1987, speculation grew that it would only be a matter of time before Routemasters were to be seen on the streets of Southampton. Indeed, during May 1987 the Stagecoach Group once more started a series of Routemaster purchases which were all placed into store at the former Hampshire Bus Overhaul Works at Barton Park, Eastleigh. However, it was with Southampton City-Bus that RM operation was to commence when, from Friday 29 May 1987 traditional crew operation was restored to the streets of the city on new service 16 between the centre and the vast Millbrook Estate.

The acquisition and subsequent entry into service by City-Bus's Routemasters was a particularly rapid operation and was primarily in direct response to the antics of the newly formed Southern Vectis subsidiary, Solent Blueline, who had launched a predatory strike on some of City-Bus's traditional and most lucrative services a few days earlier. The Blueline fleet comprised of a motley collection of Bristol VRs of varying ages, but significantly all carried a conductor. Initially, Southampton City-Bus acquired 12 Leyland engined Routemasters although only six buses were required for the 16. All were painted in standard Southampton red (a shade slightly darker than London) with off white relief. Large City-Bus fleetnames were fitted and black and yellow vinyls were applied extolling the virtues of the service and encouraging passengers to 'hop on at the back'.

The balance of Southampton's Routemasters entered service from Friday 3 August when crew operation was introduced to routes 17A and 23. Route 17A operated from Millbrook to Weston via the City Centre, whilst the 23 operated between Thornhill and the City Centre. This second batch of RMs featured the same red and off white livery but the City-Bus fleetnames carried were considerably smaller. From this date all 12 of Southampton's Routemasters were in service and four months' stability followed before another route restructuring took place.

A most significant event took place in October 1987 which effectively removed a potential competitor from the Southampton scene. In a surprise move Stagecoach sold the entire Southampton-based operation of Hampshire Bus to Southern Vectis who promptly amalgamated it with their own Solent Blueline operation. Included in the deal were approximately 80 vehicles but the Routemasters at Barton Park were retained and subsequently travelled north to join the Glasgow-based fleet. The sale to Southern Vectis did not include the existing Hampshire Bus Depot and Coach Station sites, which were subsequently sold for redevelopment to an outside party under a fairly controversial business deal which netted a considerably higher financial return for Stagecoach than the acquisition of the entire Hampshire Bus Company had cost them in the first place!

Following Hampshire Bus's withdrawal from Southampton, both Southampton City-Bus and Solent Blueline services were once more extensively revised in January 1988. As far as the sphere of Routemaster operation was concerned, routes 16 and 23 were both withdrawn, the 16 being partially replaced by an extension of route 17A and the provision of a new service numbered 17B. Both of these routes allowed greater penetration of the Millbrook Estate and the provision of a loop working to serve the large Lordshill area. Route 17A operated via Aldermoor to Lordshill whilst the 17B operated via Maybush. Route numbers were changed on arrival at Lordshill, thus giving the impression that each half of the loop was served by an individual service.

A loop working also exists at the Weston end of the service but in this case all buses operate clockwise around the loop, on some occasions route numbers are changed here as well! The 17A and 17B services comprise the present day Southampton City-Bus Routemaster network and 12 RMs are needed for their operation. Somewhat surprising is the fact that of the 12 Routemasters operating today only six remain of the existing batch. In fact, City-Bus have 23 Routemasters in stock at the time of writing, although never more than 12 have even been licensed at any one time.

The original batch of Southampton Routemasters were all obtained in May 1987 and were allocated fleet numbers from 402–413, the fleet number 401 being carried by the company's preserved AEC Regent V. This bus carried sign-writing proclaiming itself to be 'Southampton's last crew operated bus!' In this guise it occasionally made appearances alongside the newly acquired Routemasters on route'16. A further RM was obtained in June 1987 primarily for spare parts and was never allocated a fleet number, whilst another acquisition took place in September 1987. This particular bus (RM820) was finished in all over red livery with no off white relief, and was allocated the fleet number 414. Early in 1988 it was placed into service, replacing 403 (RM1993) which was subsequently sold for preservation. The new owner intends to keep the vehicle in its Southampton colour scheme.

Five more RMs were purchased in November 1987 and the intention was that they would be used by the newly formed, part City-Bus owned 'Red Admiral' subsidiary which was based in Portsmouth. In the event Red Admiral's vehicle requirements have been best served by minibuses and, following the sale of municipally-owned Portsmouth City Transport to a consortium of which Southampton City-Bus have a part share, it now seems that Routemaster operation in Portsmouth is extremely unlikely. These five vehicles have never been allocated fleet numbers and are now believed to be up for sale without ever seeing service under City-Bus ownership.

During the early part of 1988 another five buses were taken into stock and these were finished in the same all over red livery style initiated by 414 (RM820). These five RMs were allocated fleet numbers 415–419 and all entered service during April 1988, replacing five earlier acquisitions upon which considerable expenditure would have to be incurred in order to bring them up to standard following expiry of their PSV certificates; these five vehicles are also currently up for sale.

No doubt, when these additional Routemasters were obtained plans existed for their operation alongside the original batch and not for replacement of PSV expired buses. Following a recent announcement by Southampton City-Bus that a number of new double deck buses are on order for delivery late in 1988, and that future Routemaster requirements are currently under review, it does seem to imply that the original appeal of Routemaster operation appears to have waned. Along with the fact that a number of RMs are currently up for sale, it could well be that Routemaster operation in Southampton is drawing to a close.

City-Bus's first Routemasters were fitted with large fleetnames and vinyls promoting route 16. Such was the rush for the vehicles to enter service that temporary destination blinds were produced as seen here on Southampton 405 (RM1363) at Shirley a few weeks after introduction. *(Peter Relf)*

Following a restructuring of services in August 1987 blind sets were produced in Johnston style. As the buses were no longer route-bound the route 16 vinyls were replaced by something a little more general in terms of marketing. Southampton 404 (RM2037) is seen in the City Centre on route 17A. *(Steve Fennell)*

Southampton 402 (RM1793) is seen at Shirley on route 17B, introduced in January 1988. *(Steve Fennell)*

Southampton City-Bus services which see scheduled Routemaster operation

17A: Weston–Woolston–Southampton City Centre–
Shirley–Millbrook–Aldermoor–Lordshill
(Mon.–Sat., not evenings)

17B: Weston–Woolston–Southampton City Centre–
Shirley–Millbrook–Maybush–Lordshill
(Mon.–Sat., not evenings)

Southampton City-Bus Routemaster Fleetlist

City-Bus Fleet No.	RM No.	Registration Number
402	RM1793	793DYE
404	RM2037	ALM37B
406	RM564	WLT564
410	RM1539	539CLT
411	RM1543	543CLT
413	RM2059	ALM59B
414	RM820	WLT820
415	RM1682	682DYE
416	RM1871	ALD871B
417	RM1969	ALD969B
418	RM1654	654DYE
419	RM1546	546CLT

The following are withdrawn and still in stock pending disposal:

405	RM1363	363CLT
407	RM2005	ALM5B
408	RM1713	713DYE
409	RM2011	ALM11B
412	RM2043	ALM43B

The following was withdrawn in approx. 2/88 and sold 6/88:

403	RM1993	ALD993B

The following were intended for the Red Admiral operation in Portsmouth, but are believed to be currently available for sale. No fleet numbers were ever allocated.

RM969	WLT969
RM1404	404CLT
RM1889	ALM889B
RM2018	ALM18B
RM2026	ALM26B

Liveries

402–407 are red with off white relief and carry large 'City-Bus' fleetnames.

408–413 are red with off white relief and carry small 'City-Bus' fleetnames.

414–419 are all over red and carry small 'City-Bus' fleetnames.

Notes

403 was the first RM to be withdrawn, subsequently sold for preservation. Replaced in the operational fleet by 414 in approx. 2/88.

405, 407, 408, 409 and 412 were withdrawn so as to avoid costly recertification work. Replaced in operational fleet by 415–419 in 4/88.

RM1921 was also acquired but has been broken up and used for spare parts.

The second batch of City-Bus Routemasters, introduced from August 1987, featured much smaller fleetnames as illustrated here on Southampton 411 (RM1543). The bus is seen at Woolston. *(Steve Fennell)*

Some crews, when operating on route 17A, prefer to show Aldermoor as opposed to Lordshill so as to provide a second indication as to which way around the loop they are travelling. Southampon 408 (RM1713) carries a good load out of Shirley on an evening peak journey in March 1988. *(Steve Fennell)*

Later RM purchases were finished in all over red livery without any off-white relief at all. The first to be so treated was Southampton 414 (RM820) which is seen at Southampton Station. This bus replaced 403 (RM1993) which was withdrawn and subsequently sold for preservation. *(Steve Fennell)*

In April 1988 five further RMs entered service, replacing some of the earlier batch whose 'certificates of fitness' had expired. These five buses were also finished in all over red livery and Southampton 419 (RM1546) is seen near Lordshill shortly after introduction to service. *(Steve Fennell)*

Another of the 'all red' batch, Southampton 415 (RM1682), is seen in Southampton City Centre. *(Steve Fennell)*

Stagecoach/Cumberland Motor Services Ltd

Cumberland Motor Services commenced Routemaster operation from 26 October 1987 when eight AEC engined vehicles were obtained and allocated to Carlisle Depot for use on cross-city service 61. This route links the vast Morton Park and Harraby East estates with the City Centre. When first introduced the RMs operated throughout the evenings. Even the Sunday service was crew operated, albeit using a Fleetline as the capacity of an RM was insufficient to cater for the traffic on offer, particularly during the evening period. One RM did operate on Sundays however, covering meal relief periods on the normally OPO local services 60, 70 and 72, but since June 1988 these workings have themselves been converted to driver only operation as has the evening and Sunday services on route 61.

The introduction of the Routemasters in Carlisle commenced shortly after the acquisition of Cumberland Motor Services by the Stagecoach Group. Various fleet alterations took place between Stagecoach owned companies at the time and gave rise to accusations by the local MP that the average age of the Carlisle based fleet was being deliberately increased by the new owners and sighted the RMs and various former Hampshire Bus DMSs which had been transferred in as the prime examples of this policy. The local press made great mention of this which led to a response from Stagecoach management that a number of brand new buses were on order and some of these were intended for the Cumberland fleet. Whether these new acquisitions will be used to effect replacement of the Routemaster fleet remains to be seen. However, the return of crew operation has been highly praised by some of the offending MP's constituents which must surely prove something!

The Cumberland Routemaster fleet was obtained from two different sources. Six vehicles were obtained from Kelvin Scottish when that company undertook a major fleet reduction in summer 1987. The other two were obtained direct from London Buses. Of note is the fact that two of the fleet, RMs 1933 and 1983 (CMS 904 and 903 respectively), both carried special liveries whilst in London service during 1983 as part of the LT jubilee celebrations. All vehicles are finished in CMS red with a vertical diagonally situated caramel stripe.

This livery, however, is set to change to the Stagecoach corporate style as illustrated in the centre colour section. Stagecoach management have decided that all vehicles operated by companies within the group should be to the same styling so as to effect company to company vehicle transfers with the minimum of fuss. Local identity fleetnames will be retained however.

CMS services which see scheduled Routemaster operation

60A: City Centre–Botcherby–Harraby East (two Mon.–Fri. a.m. peak journeys only)

61: Morton Park–Wigton Road–City Centre–London Road–Harraby East (Mon.–Sat., not evenings)

61A: Morton Park–Morton School–Wigton Road–City Centre–London Road–Harraby East (schooldays only– one a.m. and one p.m. journey only)

CMS Routemaster Fleetlist

CMS Fleet No.	RM No.	Registration Number
900	RM713	WLT713
901	RM2024	ALM24B
902	RM1941	ALD941B
903	RM1983	ALD983B
904	RM1933	ALD933B
905	RM706	WLT706
906	RM875	WLT875
907*	RM824	WLT824

CMS Nos 900 and 901 (RMs 713 and 2024) were obtained from London Buses. The remainder were obtained from Kelvin Scottish.

* indicates that bus carries early body with non opening front upper deck windows.

An additional RM joined the fleet in March 1988 when RM560 was transferred in from the Stagecoach Magicbus subsidiary in Glasgow. This bus was used for driver training duties only and has since been returned. Notable was the fact that it was Leyland engine equipped, re-registered from WLT560 to EDS50A, and finished in all over base white livery.

Facing page top:
CMS903 (RM1983) is perhaps best remembered for the livery once carried in London in 1983 as part of the LT jubilee celebrations–all over gold! Initially sold to Kelvin Scottish, the bus passed to Cumberland, along with five others from the Kelvin batch in summer 1987. Behind is another former London vehicle, DMS2194, transferred to the Cumberland fleet from Hampshire Bus. *(Steve Fennell)*

Facing page bottom:
CMS900 (RM713) is seen in Morton Park. This bus was obtained direct from London Buses. *(Steve Fennell)*

cms Carlislebus
61
Wigton Road
City Centre
London Road
MORTON PARK
903
903
cms Carlislebus
ALD983B
70
RICHARDS

cms Carlislebus
61
Wigton Road
City Centre
London Road
HARRABY EAST
900
900
cms Carlislebus
WISE-BUY
TO LET
WLT 713

Generally speaking, buses on route 61 take their stand time in Carlisle City Centre but sometimes if there is time to spare buses pause for a few minutes halfway around the Harraby loop. CMS901 (RM2024) is seen at this point. This was the other CMS Routemaster to be obtained direct from London Buses, the remainder came from Kelvin Scottish. *(Steve Fennell)*

Again in Harraby East, CMS905 (RM706) works the 61A school journey. *(Steve Fennell)*

CMS904 (RM1933) arrives at Morton Park. This bus also appeared in a special livery in London in 1983 in connection with the LT jubilee celebrations, in this case a version of the actual 1933 livery style. The coincidence that the vehicle's fleetnumber was 1933 should not be overlooked. *(Steve Fennell)*

Some Sunday crew work was scheduled at Carlisle but this has recently ceased. CMS907 (RM824) is seen at Garlands Hospital on route 72. This vehicle is the only one of the CMS batch to carry an early body with non opening upper deck front windows. *(Steve Fennell)*

Stagecoach/United Counties Omnibus Co. Ltd

Originally billed as a nine month trial, United Counties Routemasters took to the streets of Bedford from 1 February 1988 on cross town service 101. Operating from Woodside in the north of the town to Kempston in the south, the service is an amalgamation of the former 100 and 101 routes which operated in alternate directions around the Kempston loop. On RM conversion the anticlockwise working (route 100) was discontinued, all buses operating in a clockwise direction as route 101. Limited peak hour projections exist at both ends of the service and these are detailed fully in the route working list below. It certainly appears that crew operation in Bedford is here to stay, at least for the foreseeable future, such is the popularity of the service.

Following on from Bedford was the introduction of RMs to Corby. Concurrent with the introduction of crew operation was a complete restructuring of the town service network with enhanced frequencies on many routes. Corby itself is well served by many taxi operators, and it is the taxis that hold the highest market share of the traffic on offer. The introduction of the RMs was seen as a significant attack on the taxi market but whether such measures are successful or not remains to be seen! Routemaster operation commenced in Corby from Monday 11 April 1988. The main operation centres on route 1 which is a fairly short 'dumbbell' pattern service linking the estates at Beanfield, Welland Vale and Shire Lodge with the Town Centre. Routemasters are also allocated to evening services 2A and 2C which are circular services linking most of the estates with each other and the Town Centre (A and C standing for anticlockwise and clockwise). At one stage RM operation ceased on these services due to problems with rowdiness and crew operated Bristol VRs were substituted. Just recently the RMs have returned, which hopefully suggests that the problems have been solved. Routemasters can also be seen on route 4, the vast majority of which is crew operated. This service links the remaining industrial sites with various estates and the Town Centre, and is in fact a conglomeration of different routes grouped under the same service number. Whether the Corby Routemasters are as successful as their Bedford colleagues remains to be seen. Loadings are certainly variable but whether they are sufficient to justify a crew of two is open to speculation!

Apart from one example, all of UCOC's Routemasters were obtained direct from London Buses and are AEC engined examples. The 'odd man out' is UCOC No. 717 (RM504) which was transferred from the Stagecoach Magicbus fleet. This bus is currently fitted with a Leyland engine and has been re-registered with a non-London registration. It is officially classed as a spare vehicle and may see service at either Bedford or Corby Depots. UCOC's livery is a very attractive green based scheme with orange, yellow and cream relief. It is widely considered to be one of the smartest liveries to adorn a Routemaster in the provinces and regrettably is doomed to an early retirement. Stagecoach Group management have decreed that all future repaints must adopt the Stagecoach corporate style as illustrated in the centre colour section. Local identity fleetnames will continue to be displayed, the idea being that vehicles can be easily transferred from one company to another with the minimum of attention. It is believed that UCOC717 (RM504) will be the last UCOC vehicle to be painted in the former green livery style.

UCOC services
which see scheduled Routemaster operation

1: Beanfield–Corby Town Centre–Welland Vale– Shire Lodge
(Mon.–Sat. not evenings)

2A: Corby Town Centre–Welland Vale–Kingsthorpe– Beanfield–Corby Town Centre
(Mon.–Sat. evenings only)

2C: Corby Town Centre–Beanfield–Kingsthorpe– Welland Vale–Corby Town Centre
(Mon.–Sat. evenings only)

4: Corby Industrial Service
(Mon.–Fri., no mid morning service, and Sats early a.m.)

101: Kempston–Bedford Town Centre–Woodside
One Mon.–Fri a.m. peak journey commences from Renhowe. One Mon.–Fri. a.m. peak journey commences from Stewartby, whilst one Mon.–Fri. p.m. peak journey is extended to Stewartby
(Mon.–Sat. not evenings)

161: Stewartby–Kempston–Bedford Town Centre
(one Mon.–Fri. p.m. peak journey only)

Stagecoach/UCOC Routemaster Fleetlist

UCOC Fleet No.	RM No.	Registration Number	Allocation
701	RM512	WLT512	B
702	RM528	WLT528	B
703*	RM682	WLT682	B
704	RM908	WLT908	B
705	RM1068	68CLT	B
706	RM1647	647DYE	B
707	RM2122	CUV122C	B
708	RM2192	CUV192C	B
709	RM51	VLT51	C
710	RM255	VLT255	C
711	RM980	WLT980	C
712	RM985	WLT985	C
713	RM1224	224CLT	C
714	RM1685	685DYE	C
715	RM1820	820DYE	C
716	RM2060	ALM60B	C
717	RM504	EDS48A†	B/C

Allocation codes: B=Bedford   C=Corby

* Indicates that bus carries early body with non opening front upper deck windows.

† Originally registered WLT504.

RMs 167, 410, 2040 and 2095 were also acquired for spare parts only.

United Counties first Routemasters entered service in February 1988 from Bedford Depot on route 101. Seen at the Woodside terminus is UCOC701 (RM512). *(Steve Fennell)*

UCOC708 (RM2192) is seen at Putnoe. In their marketing UCOC make great mention of the merits of crew operation. Every available advertising space on the bus being used for this purpose. *(Steve Fennell)*

UCOC705 (RM1068) pauses in Queens Drive, Putnoe en route to Woodside. From all accounts the introduction of Routemasters to Bedford has been an extremely successful exercise.
(Steve Fennell)

These two views show in detail the extensive advertising that the Bedford RMs carry in order to market themselves effectively. Note the UCOC fleetnumber plate on the rear panel of RM908. All Bedford based buses carry a blue backed plate whilst those at Corby have a yellow backing.
(Steve Fennell)

The introduction of RMs to Corby took place a few months after Bedford, and of the additional vehicles required most were prepared for service at Bedford Depot. In ex-London condition, RM255, later to become UCOC710 awaits its turn for preparation work alongside some other more prosaic members of UCOC's fleet. *(Steve Fennell)*

Corby's Routemasters generally operate on route 1 with evening and peak hour ventures on to other services. UCOC715 (RM1820) is seen in Studfall Avenue. Similar advertising to the Bedford fleet is carried, although obviously locally orientated. *(Steve Fennell)*

The advertising does not sit so happily on buses with exterior illuminated advert panels and it is apparent that someone has been busy with a pair of scissors in this particular case! UCOC716 (RM2060) is illustrated at Beanfield on route 1. *(Steve Fennell)*

Evening services 2A and 2C provide links between most of the outlying estates and the Town Centre. Most surprisingly, crew operation is employed on these services and UCOC713 (RM1224) is seen near Kingsthorpe on the clockwise working. Note that the bus seems to have missed out on the publicity stakes and shows what a difference in appearance the advertisements make. *(Steve Fennell)*

The 'odd man out' in the United Counties Routemaster fleet is No. 717. This bus was transferred in from the Stagecoach Magicbus fleet and initially operated in all over base white livery. Also unusual is the fact that the vehicle carries a Leyland engine whereas all other UCOC RMs are AEC equipped. Since this photograph was taken, in April 1988, 717 has received full United Counties green livery and is believed to be the last bus in the fleet to receive these colours, all further repaints being in Stagecoach corporate style of white with red, blue and orange stripes. Officially classed as a spare vehicle, 717 may see service at either Bedford or Corby Depots and its fleet-number plate has the backing colour split diagonally to signify its status. Seen here at Weldon North, the bus is operating on Corby Industry service 4. *(Russell Upcraft)*

On 24 July 1988 Cambus Ltd, based in Cambridge, held a vintage bus day in Peterborough and as well as a most interesting collection of Bristol Loddekas and the like, two United Counties Routemasters from Corby Depot were also loaned for the day. UCOC714 operated on Town Service 51 and is illustrated at Westwood. Later in the day the bus returned to Corby operating on route X65. *(Steve Fennell)*

The other UCOC Routemaster to operate in Peterborough was 715 (RM1820) which spent the day on route 52. With its 'on hire to Cambus' sticker clearly showing, the Routemaster is illustrated on stand at Yaxley. *(Steve Fennell)*

Burnley & Pendle Transport Co. Ltd

Following a two day evaluation of Blackpool Transport's RM1735 in February 1988 (albeit not in public service), Burnley & Pendle quickly took the decision to acquire and operate a small number of Routemasters. Five buses were initially obtained, four for service and one as a source of spare parts and, unlike the evaluation vehicle which was fitted with a Leyland engine, all were AEC equipped vehicles. Such was the desire for Burnley's newly-acquired Routemasters to enter service that only one vehicle had received Burnley livery prior to the introduction date of 14 March 1988; the remainder entering service in their former London colours.

Since deregulation Burnley and Pendle have been experiencing a considerable amount of competition from a number of local independents. In particular, the Burnley to Colne corridor has perhaps received the most attention from these operators and, not surprisingly, it is on this section of route that the majority of Routemaster activity takes place.

Burnley have marketed the RMs as 'EastEnders' after the well known television series, this also drawing attention to the London connection associated with the buses. Each vehicle, following repaint into Burnley livery, has been named after a well known character in the series and these names are displayed on the front advertisement panels.

Initial results following the re-introduction of crew operation have been encouraging and on bus revenue has seen a small percentage increase. During August 1988 another RM was acquired, the result of which may well be a slight expansion in the level of crew operation.

Burnley & Pendle services which see scheduled Routemaster operation

19: Burnley–Marsden Cross–Nelson–Colne

23: Burnley–Brierfield–Nelson–Colne

25: Colne–Nelson–Brierfield–Burnley

All services operate Mon.–Sat., not evenings.

Additionally, a Routemaster occasionally operates on route 20 between Burnley and Padiham.

Burnley & Pendle Routemaster Fleetlist

Burnley Fleet No.	RM No.	Registration Number	Name
180	RM2180	CUV180C	Queen Vic
184	RM2114	CUV114C	Wicksy
186	RM2156	CUV156C	Dirty Den
187	RM2087	CUV187C	Dot Cotton
–	RM2133*	CUV133C	–

Additionally, RM2013 was acquired for spare parts.

* At the time of going to press (19 October 1988) this bus had yet to be allocated a fleetnumber. Presumably it will take the vacant 183 slot.

Burnley & Pendle's small fleet of Routemasters are marked as 'EastEnders' with each vehicle named after a character in the series. Burnley 186 (RM2156) alias 'Dirty Den' is seen near Nelson. This bus was the first Burnley Routemaster to be repainted into the company livery. *(Steve Fennell)*

Still in London livery, Burnley 180 (RM2180) arrives at Burnley Bus Station. This bus has subsequently been named 'Queen Vic'.
(Steve Fennell)

Burnley 184 (RM2114) leaves Colne Bus Station. A vehicle of one of Burnley's main competitors ('Tyrer Tours') is seen in the background.
(Steve Fennell)

East Yorkshire Motor Services Ltd

East Yorkshire commenced Routemaster operation from Tuesday 3 May 1988, when seven vehicles were allocated to the company's Hull Depot for use on routes 56 and 56A between Hull City Centre and the Longhill Estate area. These particular services were chosen for a return to crew operation primarily because of the very tight running time prevailing and the fact that the routes themselves generate a considerable amount of short distance traffic. All in all, an ideal environment for a crew operated service! Had driver only operation been retained then an additional vehicle would have been required to maintain the same level of service as was proposed using the Routemasters.

The revival of crew operation coincided with the revival of East Yorkshire's traditional dark blue and primrose livery. Such was the timescale to receive the buses into service that three different sources were used to have the vehicles repainted. Five were treated by East Kent Engineering, one by London Buses Edgware Garage and one by East Yorkshire themselves. Initially, some buses entered service without the white roof band which was part of the original colour scheme. All had received this refinement a few weeks later however.

East Yorkshire have no plans to extend the sphere of Routemaster operation and the whole exercise is being kept under close scrutiny. In common with the majority of other RM operators, only the Mon.–Sat. daytime service is crew operated. The evening and Sunday service being provided by driver only operated vehicles.

**East Yorkshire services
which see scheduled Routemaster operation**

56: Hull Station–Holderness Road–Longhill ASDA Store
(Mon.–Sat., not evenings)

56A: Hull Station–Holderness Road–Longhill Fleet Estate
(Mon.–Sat., not evenings)

56D: Hull Station–Alfred Gelder St–Holderness Road–
Longhill ASDA Store/Fleet Estate
(two Mon.–Sat. early a.m. journeys only–
56D is not carried on the destination blinds)

East Yorkshire Routemaster Fleetlist

EY Fleet No.	RM No.	Registration Number
801	RM732	WLT732
802	RM798	WLT798
803	RM871	WLT871
804	RM982	WLT982
805	RM1041	41CLT
806	RM1271	271CLT
807	RM1366	366CLT

RM846 was also acquired for spare parts only.

East Yorkshire 807 (RM1366) is seen at Fleet Estate in full traditional East Yorkshire livery of dark blue and primrose, including the white roof band. *(Steve Fennell)*

Initially, some of the East Yorkshire RMs operated without the additional livery refinement on the roof panels as illustrated here on East Yorkshire 802 (RM798) at the ASDA Store at Longhill. *(Steve Fennell)*

The East Yorkshire Routemaster fleet benefited by the provision of full London style destination blind sets as illustrated on the rear of EY802 (RM798) at Longhill ASDA. Note that the terminal point also appears on the rear via point screen. *(Steve Fennell)*

EY804 (RM982) leaves Fleet Estate on the 56A varient of the service. This bus also has yet to be fully treated to East Yorkshire's livery. *(Steve Fennell)*

A Routemaster excursion programme is operated by East Yorkshire, hence the reason for EY801 (RM732) being found at the 1988 Sandtoft Transport Centre's annual gathering. Alongside is something a little more traditional from the former East Yorkshire fleet, a Willowbrook bodied AEC Regent V with the distinctive style of bodywork which enabled double deck vehicles to negotiate safely the famous Bar at Beverley. *(Steve Fennell)*

Greater Manchester Buses

Manchester's first involvement with Routemaster operation can be traced as far back as March 1963 when RM1414 was loaned to the then 'Manchester Corporation Transport' for evaluation trials from the company's Parrs Wood Garage. Although Manchester was highly impressed with the vehicle's performance none was purchased due primarily to the high initial cost of the bus compared with other offerings at the time, such as the latest generation of rear engined double decks that were making an impression on the market throughout the early 1960s.

Twenty-five years later and after much significant company change and restructuring, Routemasters were introduced to the city of Manchester by the present incumbent operator, Greater Manchester Buses. Since deregulation in October 1986 it is fair to say that Manchester has probably seen more competition on its streets than most other areas. Ironically, the sale of surplus Greater Manchester vehicles has enabled competitors to equip their fleets with relatively modern well maintained buses at very little cost and it is these very vehicles that GM Buses now find themselves in competition with!

The Wilmslow Road in Manchester is one such hotbed of competition with local independent 'Walls' and the North Western Roadcar Company providing the additional presence. Not surprisingly, therefore, it is on the Wilmslow Road that the Routemasters are to be found!

Introduced from Monday 5 September 1988, the RMs were put to work on a new service numbered 143 linking Piccadilly Bus Station with West Didsbury. The 143 has replaced the short working journeys between these two points on route 43 and the different number has been given to distinguish between the more normal OPO service and this new crew operated facility. Route 143 is, therefore, 100% RM operated and operates Mon.–Fri. from 07.45 until midnight. On Saturdays the service starts up about 09.15 hrs and finishes at the Mon.–Fri. times

The whole operation plays strongly on the London theme with vehicles retaining latter day London livery and the service being marketed as the 'Piccadilly Line'. Even the fleetname is based very loosely on the LT bullseye symbol as can be seen from the accompanying photographs. To add to the London image full Johnstone style destination blinds have been supplied.

Ironically, when RM1414 was evaluated some 25 years ago one of the routes upon which it operated served the Wilmslow Road. Who would have thought that the very type of bus that was so firmly rejected in 1963 would be seen to be such an effective marketing tool in the competitive environment of the 1980s? Circumstances indeed do change!

GM Buses services
which are scheduled for Routemaster operation

143: Piccadilly–Rusholme–Fallowfield–
West Didsbury
(Mon.–Sat. all day operation)

GM Buses Routemaster Fleetlist

GM Fleet No.	RM No.	Registration Number
2200	RM 2200	CUV200C
2201	RM1136	136CLT
2202	RM1776	776DYE
2203	RM1604	604DYE
2204	RM2162	CUV162C
2205	RM1618	618DYE
2206	RM378	WLT378
2207	RM429	WLT429
2208	RM698	WLT698
2209	RM1807	807DYE

Marketed as the 'Piccadilly Line', it is only natural that Manchester's new Routemaster service should commence from Piccadilly Bus Station. Seen on stand at Piccadilly is GM Buses 2200, coincidently RM2200. Note the GM Buses symbol on the side panels; its adaptation from the LT bullseye being very apparent. *(Steve Fennell)*

GM Buses 2202 (RM1776) arrives at the West Didsbury terminus. It is intended that all RMs will eventually carry their London number as well as their new GM Buses identity. The London numbers will be sited in the traditional position, the GM Buses numbers are situated over the fuel filler cap. *(Steve Fennell)*

West Didsbury stand lends itself to photography very well as it is off the main road and is fairly quiet. GM Buses 2201 (RM1136) pauses briefly before returning to the City Centre. *(Steve Fennell)*

GM Buses 2204 (RM2162) sets off from West Didsbury. Note the extensive advertising on the buses to promote the service. Manchester Routemasters are all allocated to Princess Road Garage. *(Steve Fennell)*

Southend Transport Ltd

outhend Transport, although one of the latest undertakings to purchase Routemasters, is certainly no newcomer to their operation. Southend's first experience with Routemasters came in February 1987 when RM1571 was borrowed from a preservationist and placed into service on a wide cross-section of Southend's services. This particular bus was originally sold to Stagecoach as one of their intended fleet for the deregulated market in Glasgow. It was, however, 'swopped' with a preserved Northern General example from the present owner.

Later the same year, to combat a shortage of serviceable vehicles, four RMs were hired from the 'London Coaches' subsidiary of London Buses and were used primarily on route 1 (Southend–Rayleigh); ironically, the 1 has been converted to Routemaster operation with Southend's latest purchases! The hired fleet never exceeded four vehicles on loan at any one time, although five different RMs were used during the period of the hire. These buses, RMs 237, 307, 377, 450 and 545, all operated in full traditional London livery, carrying full advertising for the 'Original London Sightseeing Tour'. The period of loan lasted from 25 November to 19 December 1987. RM545, since being returned to London, has been chosen as the test-bed for the evaluation of a DAF engine and the vehicle is currently undergoing service trials.

Southend Transport took the decision to purchase Routemasters during summer 1988, following a reappraisal of the fleet. Twelve buses have been acquired, all AEC engined examples, and delivery from London commenced during August 1988. Ironically, the RMs are being used to replace Southend's batch of former London Fleetlines of the infamous DMS marque!

Routemaster operation commenced from Saturday 3 September when one bus entered service on route 29 (Southend–Eastwood). As further RMs became available so their use on route 29 increased. Included within the 29 allocation were some scheduled evening peak journeys on routes 23, 23A and 23B (Leigh Station–Eastwood), although these have now ceased following a schedule alteration, the last day of operation being Friday 30 September. From the following Monday (3 October), Routemasters were introduced to routes 1 and 3A, although initially insufficient were available for a full allocation. In common with the majority of other Routemaster operators, crew operation is restricted to the Mon.–Sat. daytime service only.

The livery of the Southend Routemaster fleet is based upon that introduced to the company's Minibuses. Buses carry a light blue and white scheme with a narrow red band situated just below the upper deck windows. One Routemaster (RM172) has been adopted as a 'Showbus' and is to have many of its former London refinements added: brake cooling grills, full depth heater intake grill, etc. RM172, coincidentally, is the only example in Southend's fleet to carry an early body with non opening front upper deck windows, this being the prime reason why this vehicle has been chosen.

Southend Transport services which see scheduled Routemaster operation

1: Southend–Hadleigh–Rayleigh Station
(Mon.–Sat., not evenings)

3A: Southend–Hadleigh–Canvey
(Mon.–Sat., not evenings)

7: Southend–Rochford–Golden Cross
(Mon.–Fri. p.m. schoolday duplicate journeys only)

9A: Southend–Southend Airport–Eastwood
(one return Mon.–Sat. p.m. journey only)

29: Southend–Westcliff Schools–Eastwood
(Mon.–Sat., not evenings)

63: Southend–Temple Sutton
(one return Sat. early a.m. journey only)

Southend Transport RM Fleetlist

Southend Fleet No.	RM No.	Registration Number
101*	RM12	OYM413A
102†	RM172	VLT172
103	RM577	WLT577
104	RM797	WLT797
105	RM937	WLT937
106	RM949	WLT949
107	RM993	WLT993
108	RM1061	61CLT
109	RM1183	183CLT
110	RM2034	ALM34B
111	RM2101	ALM101B
112	RM2124	CUV124C

* Originally registered VLT12. This mark is now carried by London Buses Metrobus M1437.

† Indicates that bus carries early body with non opening front upper deck windows.

Top: **The first Routemaster to see service in Southend was privately owned RM1571 in February 1987. Still in ex-London condition, the Routemaster is seen at Canewdon on route 12.** *(Russell Upcraft)*

Middle: **Once Southend acquired their own Routemasters their use on routes 23/A/B was very short-lived, lasting only a little over three weeks. The weather on the evening of 28 September was absolutely vile and the departure of the 18.00 hrs from Leigh Station coincided with a torrential downpour. Seen in the gloom at Leigh is Southend 110 (RM2034).** *(Steve Fennell)*

Bottom: **From Eastwood the bus returned to Leigh as a route 23. Southend 110 is seen performing the reverse turn at Eastwood Belgrave Road, a terminus shared with RM workings on route 29. All of Southend's Routemasters have been fitted with fluorescent lights as can be clearly seen in this photograph.** *(Steve Fennell)*

Top: The more normal RM allocations are to be found on routes 1 and 3A. Southend 111 (RM2101) is seen near Southend Victoria Station heading for Rayleigh. *(Steve Fennell)*

Middle: Southend 102 (RM172) is seen opposite the company's depot in London Road. This bus is the only plain windowed vehicle in the Southend fleet, the result of which has been the decision to adopt this vehicle as a company 'Showbus'. For this reason the vehicle retains white on black registration numbers, all others of the Southend batch being fitted with new reflective plates. Further ex-London refinements will be fitted to the bus in due course. *(Steve Fennell)*

Bottom: **Most of the Hadleigh short working journeys on route 1 remain in the hands of OPO vehicles. However, a few peak hour RM workings do exist as illustrated by Southend 112 (RM2124) on stand at Hadleigh. These journeys, prior to 3 October, were numbered 1A and coincidental with the introduction of the RMs were renumbered 1. Unfortunately, the side blinds for these short workings retain 1A on them and so as to present half the blinds displaying a different route from the remainder, certain crews persist in showing 1A for these journeys. Once the offending 'A's have been removed from the sides and rears then these few workings will adopt the parent number.** *(Steve Fennell)*

Independents

Whereas the Routemaster has found many friends in a number of major operators throughout the country, much interest can be found within the independent sector where the RM has, once again, been found to be the ideal vehicle for many different operators' requirements. One slightly irritating factor within this sphere of operation has been the reluctance of certain companies to paint the vehicles in their 'house liveries'; many preferring to retain the buses in their former London colours to emphasise their parentage.

In view of the fact that many operators have perhaps only one or two buses, each company is listed in alphabetical order, with a brief resumé of their operations.

Blue Triangle
ROMFORD, ESSEX

Blue Triangle are enthusiastic operators of all things AEC and, not surprisingly, are ardent supporters of Routemaster operation. Seven vehicles comprise the present Routemaster fleet: two RMs, two RMAs, an RCL and two ex-Northern General examples, one of which has been converted to open-top configuration for London sightseeing work. At the time of going to press (18 October 1988) a number of these vehicles are in store and the operational fleet consists of the RCL, one RMA and the open-top Northern vehicle only. Fleet livery is red and cream, although the operational RMA carries a blue-based colour scheme.

Blue Triangle Routemaster Fleetlist	
RCL2239	CUV239C
RM1009	9CLT
RM1321	321CLT
RMA48	NMY631E
RMA49	NMY632E

Citilink
HULL, HUMBERSIDE

D. Coster, trading as 'Citilink', operates two RMs on local services in Hull. One vehicle was purchased from the Stagecoach Group and has recently been repainted in a very smart silver and blue scheme. The other RM was acquired direct from London Buses and, at the time of writing, is operating in rather tatty London livery. However, this bus is also due to receive the silver and blue colour scheme and by the time this is read may well be in 'Citilink' livery.

Much to Citilink's credit full Johnston style destination blinds are carried and two services are currently RM operated: the 643 which operates from Hull Station to Greatfield and the 644 from Hull Station to Bilton Grange. Originally the 644 was numbered 642 but was subsequently renumbered as 642 was omitted from the destination blinds. Both services operate Mon.–Sat.

Citilink Routemaster Fleetlist	
RM188	VLT188
RM1741	741DYE

RM188 acquired from London Buses, fitted with AEC engine.

RM1741 acquired from the Stagecoach Group, Leyland engine fitted.

Confidence
OADBY, LEICESTERSHIRE

K. M. Williams of Oadby, Leicestershire, trading as Confidence Bus & Coach Hire, operate two Routemasters. The first bus (RM655) was purchased in October 1985 with the second (RM621) being acquired the following June. Both have been repainted into Confidence livery of black and grey with red lining and mostly operate on school contract services or the Leicester University service numbered 45. This particular operation being shared with Midland Fox. Both vehicles are very smartly turned out and have been fitted with full London style destination blinds.

Confidence Fleet No.	RM No.	Registration Number
15	RM655	WLT655
17	RM621	WLT621

(Confidence Routemaster Fleetlist)

M. W. Gagg
BUNNY, NOTTINGHAMSHIRE

M. W. Gagg purchased his first RM in May 1987 direct from London Buses. Five months later a further example joined the fleet and to date these have been the sole Routemaster purchases. Both buses are maintained to a very high standard and both have been fully repainted, albeit retaining their former London livery. Gagg's more normal colour scheme being blue and white. The Routemasters can normally be found on routes 100 and 101, Nottingham–Keyworth and Nottingham–Rempstone respectively. Such was the success of these services which were awarded to Gagg under contract that certain journeys on the 101 are now registered as commercial.

Gagg Routemaster Fleetlist

RM790	WLT790
RM1314	314CLT

W. Gash & Sons Ltd
NEWARK

W. Gash purchased two RMs from London Buses in October 1986 following a somewhat rapid expansion of services following deregulation. A further Routemaster was acquired the following January and all three settled down on operation of Newark Town services, where the benefits of crew operation enabled a high standard of service to be maintained on what were very tightly timed driver only operated routes. Gash's three RMs all retained London livery, regrettably none were to receive Gash's very smart traditional two-tone green colour scheme. During March 1988 the company was sold to Yorkshire Traction and shortly after the Routemasters were replaced on town service work by Minibuses. The future role within the fleet of these three RMs is currently unclear.

Gash Routemaster Fleetlist

Gash Fleet No.	RM No.	Registration Number
RM19	RM1990	ALD990B
RM20	RM2065	ALM65B
RM21	RM757	WLT757

Verwood Transport
SHAFTESBURY, DORSET

A. Wood and R. Brown, trading as Verwood Transport, operate a varied and interesting fleet which includes three former British Airways Routemaster, latterly classified RMA by London Transport. Two RMAs were acquired during summer 1987 and both were converted so as to permit one person operation on stage carriage services. This conversion work entailed the fitting of additional mirrors and the provision of a periscope. Externally an illuminated 'Pay as you enter' sign was installed under the front nearside canopy.

Livery of these two vehicles is currently a very smart two-tone blue colour scheme with gold and black lining. A further RMA was purchased in very poor condition from PVS of Barnsley (breakers) and this has since been returned to PSV service. The bus was restored using parts from an RMC and as a result carries an RMC style destination blind display as well as an opening front driver's window, RMAs normally having a fixed screen. This bus made its service debut on Thursday 1 September 1988 and is finished in a two-tone green livery, applied in the same styling as on the blue liveried vehicles. The actual shades of green are those which London Transport formerly applied to the Green Line fleet in the mid 1960s.

Verwood operate two services on which an RMA may be seen. Route 90 operates Mon.–Fri. one return journey from Verwood, via West Moors, Poole, Bournemouth and Boscombe to Christchurch and is normally RMA operated. The other service operates Mondays and Saturdays only, again one return journey from Verwood to Christchurch but direct omitting Poole. This route is numbered 91 but only sees Routemaster operation on an ad-hoc basis.

Verwood Transport Routemaster Fleetlist

RMA11	NMY648E
RMA37	KGJ612D
RMA58	NMY655E

RMAs 11 and 58 carry blue livery, RMA37 carries green.

Confidence Coaches No. 15 (RM655) is seen at Leicester University on route 45. Midland Fox also operate this service as can be seen with a DMS and Leyland National in the background. *(Steve Fennell)*

Blue Triangle's RCL2239 is seen near Hatfield Heath on Essex County Council Service 622. This route is scheduled for RT operation but the RCL is utilised when either of the two RTs are required for maintenance. *(Steve Fennell)*

Citilink of Hull operate two RMs, one of which (RM1741) has been re-painted into a very smart blue and silver livery. Allocated the fleet number 3, this particular bus was purchased from the Stagecoach Group. Photographed at Bilton Grange. *(Russell Upcraft)*

M. W. Gagg's Routemaster fleet is seen in the company's yard at Bunny, Nottinghamshire. Livery is standard London red. *(Philip Hanwell)*